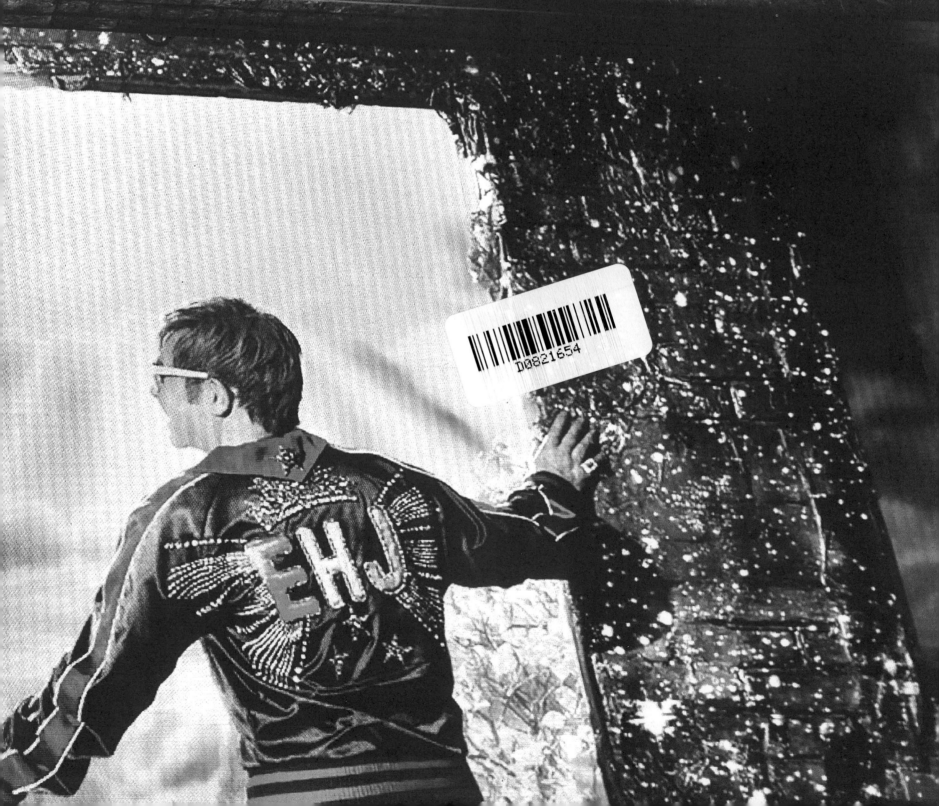

OW BRICK ROAD

ELTON JOHN

ROCKET MAN

CHRIS ROBERTS

STERLING

New York

PAGE 1: Elton John, March 1980.
PAGE 2: Elton during a portrait
session, London, 1970.
RIGHT: Elton John standing on his
piano stool during a performance,
London, 1971.

CONTENTS

INTRODUCTION
THE WINNER FROM PINNER

As Sir Elton John's years-long, marathon Farewell Yellow Brick Road tour enraptured America throughout late 2018, he apologized onstage for being unable to play everybody's personal favorites in one night. As, in most shows, he'd rattled through over two dozen of his best-loved songs, it was a humble gesture from a star whose five-decade career has moved from aspiring artist to glam-pop icon and renowned diva to rebooted, clean-living charity worker and universally applauded pop legend.

John's swansong shows kick off with a confident swagger, cameras picking out his fingers on the piano as "Bennie and the Jets" begins. The band, featuring long-time sidemen like Davey Johnstone, Ray Cooper, and Nigel Olsson, have been unafraid to rasp like younger rockers on enduring Elton anthems such as "Crocodile Rock," "All the Girls Love Alice," "The Bitch Is Back," and "Saturday Night's Alright for Fighting." The septuagenarian knight formerly known as Captain Fantastic has been paying tribute to the late Aretha Franklin, recalling how thrilled he and Bernie Taupin were when she recorded their "Border Song," and how proud he was to be one of the first white artists to perform on *Soul Train* in 1975. Films on the huge screen behind him accompany the songs, shifting from seemingly random circle-of-life imagery to vibrant, youthful dancers.

It's a smart decision that nine-tenths of the set is cherry-picked from John's prolific seventies output. Few would argue against that decade being his (and Taupin's) creative golden age. From "Rocket Man" to "Tiny Dancer" to "Philadelphia

LEFT: Elton John performs on the Farewell Yellow Brick Road Tour at the United Center, Chicago, October 26, 2018.
RIGHT: Sir Elton John performs during his Farewell Yellow Brick Road tour at the BB&T Center, Sunrise, Florida, November 23, 2018.

ABOVE: Elton John in concert at the Omni Coliseum, Atlanta, Georgia, July 16, 1976.
RIGHT: On stage at the Hammersmith Odeon, London, December 1973.

Freedom" to "Don't Let the Sun Go Down on Me," the writing pair—under intense pressure to deliver to a vast audience—were in some kind of zone, on some kind of fire. Even (relatively) lesser known songs from that era like "Indian Sunset," "Levon," and "Take Me to the Pilot" make the cut, tacitly acknowledging that they are more beloved than later work. "Someone Saved My Life Tonight," accompanied here by an animation showing the star in full, flamboyant, peak Captain Fantastic persona, was arguably their finest ballad, although post-Diana, "Candle in the Wind" would compete for that title, as would the one that started it all off, "Your Song."

Nowadays, Elton partakes of just the one costume change between his two sets, a more restrained wardrobe whirlwind than in younger days. The second set again concurs with the general public that the early seventies were his prime, rolling through "Funeral for a Friend/Love Lies Bleeding," "Burn Down the Mission," and "Daniel." In allowing the nineties in, in the shape of "Believe," he sometimes takes a moment onstage to talk about his life and career, openly discussing his struggles with substance abuse and recalling how in Chicago thirty years ago he took the crucial step of going into rehab. Sober, gratefully, he founded the Elton John AIDS Foundation, which has raised hundreds of millions of dollars for AIDS research. The show heads into its climax with, inevitably, "I'm Still Standing," where the films onscreen flash between images from every chapter of his career. Emphasizing how far he's come and how widely he's permeated popular culture, now as much an über-celebrity as a music star, it's a window on every hall of fame. There's Elton with the Queen, Elton with the Muppets, with the Simpsons, with Cher, with Eminem, with *The Lion King* cast at the Oscars, with husband David Furnish and their two kids. It's a flamboyant farewell, but the audience wishes the yellow brick road could go on forever. And as *Rocketman*, a biopic of the star, hit cinema screens worldwide in spring 2019, it felt like Elton wanted it to as well.

This most illustrious of life stories began a long, long way from the glamour, glitz, and grandstanding of this (almost) never-ending victory lap across the world. It began, as many things don't, in the town of Pinner. As shown on TV in a 2018 Christmas television ad for the UK John Lewis department store, that's where Elton John first played the piano.

★ ★ ★

THE THING ABOUT PINNER is it's really rather nice. It might make for a better narrative to suggest that Sir Elton John CBE pulled himself up by the bootstraps from rags to riches, from a tough, challenging, deprived background to the very top of the glittering entertainment world, like an urchin Cinderella.

In the Netherlands
during the Captain
Fantastic tour of 1975.

And it's true that he wasn't an over-privileged child, and was raised primarily by his maternal grandparents. Yet to over-egg the pudding by framing picturesque Pinner as a working-class town of hard knocks would be patently untrue.

Yes, it may not have been affluent in the fifties and early sixties as Elton, or Reg, went through boyhood and adolescence, and its location amid the northwestern suburbs of London means it never competes with Kensington or Hampstead for house prices. It's not generally at the heart of cultural matters. Walk from its neat, clean station and explore its scenic, time-warped high street, wide residential avenues, and large, fresh-air-fest of a park (complete with sculpted duck pond), however, and perhaps you'll find yourself deciding Pinner might be a highly pleasant place in which to grow up.

Reg grew up at the Northwood Hills end. A wealthy part of the London borough of Harrow, Pinner was first recorded as a hamlet in 1231 as "Pinnora." The chocolate-box quaintness of St. John the Baptist Church (consecrated 1321) serves as a lid atop its high street, which has a Tudor-style pub (the Queen's Head) and Edwardian buildings aplenty. They filmed scenes for *The Theory of Everything* there. That film wasn't famous for its depictions of gritty urban realness.

Yes, it's "square." You can see how a young man would get restless. Annual street fairs, folk dancers. Perhaps there's still an image hangover from John Betjeman's 1973 film *Metro-Land*, in which it featured centrally. There are lots of 1930s Art Deco–style homes, if you walk far enough from the more generic stretch of shops, and it gets plainer towards Elton's old end. Its population is predominantly white, but that statistic's been dropping consistently since Elton's day, and diversity is increasing. It has one of the lowest crime rates in all of London. It smells of prestige. Pinner Memorial Park in 2016 opened the Heath Robinson Museum, the first in the world dedicated to the eccentric visionary painter, illustrator, satirist, and inventor of modernist contraptions, "the gadget king," who lived here on Moss Lane from 1908 to 1918.

There's still, however, no Elton John Museum. No Yellow Brick Road theme park festooned with tiny dancers and honky cats where you can light your own candle in the wind. You'd wonder if Pinner was perhaps obtusely missing a trick, but more probably Elton has his own ideas, control, and rights over if and when and where that kind of merchandising malarkey might happen. Or, possibly, Pinner is just too damn cool to go on about it, given that its former residents also include novelist Ivy Compton-Burnett, Isabella Beeton (of *Mrs. Beeton's Book of Household Management* [1861] legend), Horatio Nelson and Emma Hamilton's illegitimate daughter Horatia, and Screaming Lord Sutch (not at the same time), Children's Laureate Michael Rosen, Ronnie Barker, and David Suchet (these last two in

> ELTON'S STATISTICS BROOK LITTLE ARGUMENT: HE'S SOLD OVER 300 MILLION RECORDS. HE HAD AT LEAST ONE SONG IN THE *BILLBOARD* HOT 100 EVERY YEAR FROM 1970 TO 2001.

the same house, though, again, not at the same time). From Bob Holness to Fearne Cotton, Pinner's been home to British showbiz giants.

And music? Pinner, for all that Elton may emphasize his uniqueness, has given the world more than its fair share: Gordon, of sixties' chart-toppers Peter & Gordon, and Leslie Bricusse— best known for his long-term collaboration writing musicals with Anthony Newley, and who composed such evergreens as "Goldfinger" for Shirley Bassey, "What Kind of Fool Am I?" and "The Candy Man" for Sammy Davis Jr., "You Only Live Twice" for Nancy Sinatra, and "Feeling Good" for Nina Simone. Impressive as that is, Pinner also gave us Tony Hatch (who wrote Petula Clark's "Downtown" and, with wife Jackie Trent, Scott Walker's "Joanna" and the theme song to the Australian soap opera *Neighbours*). Bruce Welch from the Shadows lived in Pinner while wooing Olivia Newton-John, and Charlie Dore (who had a US hit in 1979 with "Pilot of the Airwaves") was born and raised here. It's quite a catalog of pop history. Is there something (else) you should know? Why yes—Simon Le Bon of Duran Duran is not, as many mistakenly assume, from Birmingham at all. Born near Pinner in Bushey, he went to Pinner County Grammar School, some years after Elton did. So this small but shapely town, twelve miles northwest of Charing Cross, has delivered a wealth of creative talent to Britain and far beyond, over-performing and underselling itself.

Yet there can be little doubt as to who is Pinner's most successful, colorful, and celebrated global export of all time. Although, to be fair, Agnes Marshall, who following a fall from a horse died in Pinner in 1905, did invent the ice cream cone. But even Agnes would concede: Pinner gave us Elton John, the original Rocket Man himself, and he's still standing. This is his song.

peers, toured like a Trojan, and named himself "The Captain," before running into exhaustion and a cocaine overdose. Never as cerebral as Bowie, as arty as Roxy, or as visceral and sexy as T. Rex, he nonetheless finessed apocalyptic American success and all-consuming fame (which all but consumed him) and then a second life, after the muse had waned, as the celebrity other celebrities want to be photographed with.

Reinventing himself as chairman of Watford Football Club (Watford is not that far from Pinner, where Reg spent many unlikely hours dreaming of becoming a footballer) and a *Morecambe and Wise* guest, he was soon a comfortable seventies fixture. The eighties tried to shake him off, and he was temporarily relegated from being king of the hill, but he hung in there and bounced back in the George Michael era with his performance at Live Aid, a famous lawsuit win in a libel case against *The Sun*, and five nights at Madison Square Garden. Oh, and he married. A woman; Renate Blauel. They divorced three years later. Oddly, for all his household-name songs, he never had a solo UK No. 1 hit until the nineties embraced "Sacrifice." Chart placings became a non-issue as he graduated from the pop scene to enjoy family-friendly stage-and-screen successes with *The Lion King* and *Billy Elliot*. Sober after undergoing rehab, he's won five Grammys, five Brits, an Oscar, a Golden Globe, and even a Tony. He was named a Commander of the British Empire in 1995, and became a Knight two years later, for "services to music and charitable services."

Those charitable services included taking a prominent role in the fight against AIDS from the late eighties; in 1992, he established the Elton John AIDS Foundation, and his annual Oscars party has helped the cause raise over $200 million. After declaring he was bisexual in 1976, then coming out as gay in 1988, he's now been married to David Furnish since 2014 (they'd entered into a civil partnership nine years earlier). He's spent even more on his highly impressive art collection than he has on flowers. (In 2000, he told the High Court of a £293,000 florists' bill: "I'm a single man. I like to spend money. It's my money to spend.")

In that strange world of A-list celebrity, he's become an Alpha; one week taking phone calls from Russian president Vladimir Putin, the next hanging with his besties the Beckhams. He continues to surprise, whether it's confirming that the biopic—*Rocketman*—is on the way (with his full support) or popping up in a self-parodying role in a commercial for Snickers bars. In January 2018, he'd announced the farewell tour, which commenced that September—and is scheduled to last for three years, longer than many pop careers.

Still grandstanding better than he ever did, surviving of course, Elton has, with shrewdness, graft, and luck, maneuvered a beloved status and fabulous life. There aren't many stars who

His is, of course, a lengthy and illustrious upward, downward, and then upward again tale. Over half a century since he first collaborated with lyricist Bernie Taupin, the pair have partnered up on more than thirty albums, seven of which became consecutive US chart-toppers. Elton's statistics brook little argument: he's sold over 300 million records. He had at least one song in the *Billboard* Hot 100 every year from 1970 to 2001. The 1997 "Candle in the Wind" reboot in honor of Princess Diana's passing is (debatably, given the lack of official figures for Bing Crosby's "White Christmas") the biggest-selling single ever, in both the UK and the US. Unforgettably, he performed it at her funeral at Westminster Abbey.

That performance, arguably, reinstated him as a national treasure after a period when it seemed his stardom had at best plateaued. His rise through the seventies had been far from "overnight"; early on, he banged out albums as if they were going out of fashion, in an era when they weren't. "Your Song" gave him the breakthrough hit; albums like *Honky Château* and *Goodbye Yellow Brick Road* got traction at different times on different sides of the Atlantic, but he got there. He galloped with the glam rock bandwagon, dressed as outrageously as any of his glittering can say they've worked with John Lennon and Tupac, Little Richard and Leon Russell, Kate Bush and Queens of the Stone Age, Leonard Cohen and, er, Blue. He's outlasted his superiors; mentored his inferiors. He's played Las Vegas residencies and Diamond Jubilee concerts at Buckingham Palace. By contrast to his many triumphs like *The Lion King* and *Billy Elliot* he's written a flop Broadway musical about a vampire and been inducted into the Rock & Roll Hall of Fame by Axl Rose. Seven decades since he popped up in Pinner, Sir Elton must be glad he didn't, to paraphrase Bernie's words, stay on the farm or listen to his old man. So let's delve into the story of the man born Reginald Kenneth Dwight, now legally named Elton Hercules John, the unlikely all-conquering showbiz god, the winner from Pinner.

LEFT: George Michael and Elton John leave Westminster Abbey following the funeral service for Diana, Princess of Wales, London, September 6, 1997.
BELOW: Elton, the winner from Pinner, relaxes listening to music, 1974.

1

THE DWIGHT STUFF

"I suppose the only regret I have about my life is that I had a bad childhood. I mean: I wasn't hit on the head every three minutes with a saucepan, but my father and mother didn't get on too well, so I didn't have too many friends or anything like that. I was very, very clammed up. I suppose I'm rebelling against that now. That's why I do all these things, because I was never allowed to go out or anything.

ELTON JOHN

For beginners, Pinner. Reginald Kenneth Dwight was born there on March 25, 1947, two years after his parents, Stanley Dwight and Sheila Eileen (née Harris), married young. Pinner Hill Road, his birthplace, goes uphill, past a clocktower, past neat, tidy gardens: it aspires, gently.

William Dwight, his great grandfather, was a cobbler. Edwin, his grandfather, was a cable factory worker based in Belvedere, Kent. Edwin and his wife, Ellen, had five sons and a daughter. The youngest son was Stanley. One of Stanley's brothers, Ted, died of tuberculosis aged thirty-four. Encouraged by a friend who'd formed a local amateur swing band, Stanley—now Stan—took up the trumpet. Meanwhile, his nephew Roy Dwight, son of Ted, was showing great promise on the football field, even if the family couldn't afford shin pads and gave him books to shove down his socks instead.

Stan became a milkman, complete with horse-drawn cart. He became musically competent enough to join the swing band the Millermen, playing popular tunes like "Me and My Shadow." On occasion they played big venues like the Lyceum Ballroom near Covent Garden. And then World War II intervened. When Stan reached an eligible age for military service, he joined the Royal Air Force, and was as stunned as his family to be told he was now a commissioned officer. This was social climbing he had not anticipated and could not fully comprehend. Officers were upper class. They were the cream of British society, not the milkmen. Understandably, Stan changed. He became accustomed to order, structure, efficiency, control; to being obeyed. "Somehow from then on," his nephew Roy has mused, "he always seemed to talk a bit louder than he needed to." This was later, inevitably, to affect his relationship with his first-born.

As the war drew to a close, he met dark-haired, petite Sheila, a clerk working at RAF Coastal Command in Northwood, Middlesex. Her father, Fred Harris, had served with the Welsh Guards in World War I. He'd then become the groundsman at Hatch End Tennis Club, a job for which he'd thought nothing of cycling a forty-mile round trip each day from his Peckham home to Hatch End and back. Eventually, Fred compromised and moved, with wife Ivy and their three children, closer to work. Via spells in nearby Kenton and Hatch End they settled at Pinner Green, in a semi-detached council house, just south of that clocktower. They were the folks who lived on the hill, overlooking Metroland as they went about daily life. It was a solid, late-thirties' house: Fred cared diligently for the two allotments in the back garden. Pinner Cricket Club was on the other side of the hedge.

Stan and Sheila married at Pinner parish church in January 1945, living with Fred and Ivy here for the first few years of their wedded . . . well, not bliss exactly. Finding a place of your own was tricky for a young couple post-war. Stan had stayed on in the Volunteer Reserve and was traveling a lot with work, so Sheila didn't mind having the company of her parents as well as her sister Win and her brother—another Reg. By the time their son (our Reg, i.e. Elton) was born in 1947, Stan, who had won promotions, was a flight lieutenant. Statistically, Stan was in another class to his own family. He'd be given postings abroad, to which Sheila would let him go alone. Elton was born in her parents' house and has recounted that he felt some bitterness towards his father from an early age. Stan was overseas when Sheila went into labor. Elton's recollection is that his dad never

PREVIOUS PAGE: Elton's first publicity pictures, Hampstead, London, January 1968.
LEFT: Reg's father, Stanley Dwight, and his second wife, Edna, 1976.

came home to see him until he was two years old. "I was two when he came home. Mother asked if he wanted to see me. He said, 'No, I'll wait till morning.' He'd been in Aden or somewhere." When there are conflicting stories and opinions about the time and nature of their very first meeting, there's bound to be trouble brewing in paradise. Photographs of the infant Reggie display golden curls somewhat in the style of Shirley Temple and, already, no shortage of costume changes.

Yet the Britain around Reg was far from colorful. Food shortages and rationing persisted; austerity held the country in its gray, demoralizing grip. For Reg, as for so many, music became an escape, a treat, fantasy. Stan and Sheila, at heart, shared the enthusiasm. Stan's stint as a trumpeter meant he retained his fondness for pre-pop 78s by American stars such as Guy Mitchell, Kay Starr, and Les Paul and Mary Ford. Young Reg would study the labels, finding these objects fascinating. The house had a piano, as did many "ordinary" homes before television took over, and Sheila encouraged Reg to bang away on it to give him something to do while she got on with housework. Legend has it that one day she turned around, startled, when the little boy, aged four, picked out by ear the melody to "The Skater's Waltz." This was no fluke: he soon displayed great aptitude. Yet Stan discouraged him. "He didn't want me to go into music and I can never understand that, because he was a trumpeter in a band," Elton said in the seventies.

With his father mostly away, further potential paternal influence was lost when grandfather Fred died when Reg was five. Fred's widow, Ivy, remarried a man named Horace, who having lost a leg during the war, walked with an artificial replacement limb. It was mother and grandmother bringing up the boy now. One neighbor has described the child as being "overprotected" and not often permitted to play with others. At four he'd started at Pinner Wood Junior, the local state primary, but a year later was removed and sent to Reddiford School, a small private school of around a hundred pupils. At six he was having private piano lessons from a Mrs. Jones. An old schoolmate has recalled asking him what he wanted to be when he grew up, and receiving the reply, "A concert pianist." Having found a role of sorts, he was called on to play piano at school events as well as during family occasions. When his older cousin Roy, the footballer, got married, with Stan as best man, Reg, a page boy, had a musical star turn. The band they'd booked were late turning up, so, Roy remembered, "Reggie was put on the piano in his little white tail suit and bow tie. He kept things going until the real band arrived." It wasn't long before observers were joking that he was the local Jerry Lee Lewis. The first blast of rock and roll hit Reg when his mother brought home breakthrough records by American rockers like Elvis Presley and Bill Haley.

The piano prodigy went on to Pinner County Grammar School and at age eleven won a junior scholarship to the Royal Academy of Music, impressing instructors with a dazzling rendition of a lengthy Handel piece. By now, however, his parents' marriage was really struggling. Stan, in his thirties, was now a squadron leader and had become less jazz trumpeter and more strict, formal RAF man. The Dwight family had now moved to their own house in the Northwood Hills area of Pinner, but so unhappy was the atmosphere in this apparently pleasant, compact, detached suburban house that Elton tended to leave it out of his life story at first when later, as a star, talking to journalists. He eventually opened up and told all.

His mother was his favorite, even if they did fall out much later in life, and she consistently supported his musical drive. According to Elton, in Philip Norman's 1992 biography, when Stan was there—which wasn't too often—there was tension and awkwardness in the air. The couple, now frosty with each other, were one of those who stay together "for the children's sake." Stan would reproach the boy for manners—not sitting up straight, speaking out of turn. Even kicking a ball around in the garden was banned for fear of damage to the rose bushes. Reggie withdrew during these times into shyness and fearful politeness. And into hours of piano practice. One of the few areas in which he and his father shared excitement was in their football fandom. They'd go together to see Watford play at Vicarage Road. Elton's subsequent love affair with the club is famous, but already he had a link with soccer-related fame. Roy

FAR LEFT: You could dress up like Liberace, 1955.
LEFT: Or holler like Jerry Lee Lewis, 1958.

Dwight, having fulfilled his youthful potential, had become a professional player and was Fulham's star center-forward. He'd scored in each of his first eight games, and Reggie loved being taken to watch him impress and attain hero status at Craven Cottage. More than once Roy arranged for Elton to have a special vantage point on the touchline. Reggie, like most young boys, eagerly wanted to emulate Roy's success, but at school he showed no skill to match his enthusiasm. He was decent at tennis, but his true talents lay closer to his briefcase full of Chopin and Brahms sheet music. When television came along, flickering and gleaming, he pondered that if he couldn't be a football star, it might be fun to be a glittering entertainer like Liberace. And Winifred Atwell's succession of piano hits, to his mind, showed that piano players didn't necessarily need to be dour, classical-oriented and furrow-browed.

As rock and roll swept across the Western world, young Reg of course absorbed its energies. He was disappointed when his father gave him, instead of something capturing the fresh new sound, an album of well-mannered jazz by George Shearing. (Elton was still moaning about that decades later.) Yet when Dad wasn't around, Sheila was playing "Rock Around the Clock" and "Hound Dog." Her boy listened with wonder. He was perhaps beginning to think that playing piano—and performing while doing so—could be a blast. You could dress up like Liberace? Holler like Presley, Haley, or Jerry Lee Lewis? Well, that might be fun. Bernie Taupin many years later alluded to this young buzz in the song "Made in England."

At Pinner County Grammar School, Elton's musical qualifications and talent were already far beyond what the teachers were accustomed to within his age group. And this was an excellent school with regard to music facilities. There was a Steinway grand in the assembly hall and the headmaster and the music teacher were both accomplished classical pianists. The history master was something of a blues buff. Reggie's Royal Academy of Music scholarship reflected well on all parties. There, he was taught on Saturday mornings for the next four years by Helen Piena. Classes took place at the Academy's Marylebone Road building. Piena has spoken of Elton's gratifying combination of flair and work ethic. "I always called him by his full name, Reginald. But he was very affectionate. He'd send me letters with kisses on the bottom. Once he sent me an embroidered skullcap from Switzerland, where he'd gone on holiday with his school." Other teachers have also said he was a model student.

Elton, with hindsight, has protested that he was less of a diligent goody-goody than that. "I kind of resented going to the Academy," he said, though he's admitted he enjoyed singing in the choir. "I was one of those children who could just about get away without practicing and still pass, scrape through the grades."

Meanwhile, at grammar school he was perceived as altogether less interesting. He didn't stand out, and his academic work was generally passed as "satisfactory" or "average." His rugby teammates have vouched that "he'd always go back in again for

One of Reg's first idols, Little Richard, 1963.

The enamored Dusty Springfield, 1964.

more." In school concerts he'd happily glide along in the middle of things without striving to stand out. (It's recorded that R. Dwight played *Petites Litanies de Jésus* by Grovlez at one concert.) There's a school photograph of him aged thirteen where, far from embracing the burgeoning Teddy boy look (Dad wouldn't stand for that), he appears as unlikely a future pop sensation as one can imagine. With his glasses, he hoped he looked like Buddy Holly. If rock and roll had entered his world as a temptation, it was now a quiet obsession. And thanks to Sheila's record collection, he was more into the rawer American styles than the softer UK crossover readings. He acquired all of Little Richard's records, and as one of his first outings to a concert went to see his new idol perform at Harrow's Granada cinema. He adored the American accents, as his subsequent vocal stylings attest. However, Sheila didn't let him go to see Jerry Lee Lewis, whose UK tour was cut short upon the disclosures concerning his marriage to his thirteen-

year-old cousin. The influence of both Little Richard and Lewis on Elton's subsequent onstage persona is blatantly obvious.

He wasn't yet too sociable, and his music lessons and practice kept him both busy and isolated. In his bedroom, when not studying, he'd curate his ever-growing record collection. "I grew up with inanimate objects as my friends," he later said with an air of melancholy. Of course, he also matured into a collector, a hoarder. He was a fan, and always would be—of music, of football and later, of photography and art.

In 1962, Stan petitioned for divorce from Sheila. Her relationship with Fred Farebrother, a local painter and decorator, was a factor. Reggie, now fourteen, could have been forgiven for being, despite his antipathy towards Stan, distressed. At the Royal Academy, he told Helen Piena he might have to forsake his scholarship, and that he wouldn't now be able to have the new piano he felt he sorely needed. However, she received a phone call from Stan telling her he could have the new piano and continue his studies. When Stan remarried eighteen months later, and his new wife Edna Clough gave birth to four boys in quick succession, Reggie's bitterness increased. His pride was hurt. His father's sudden fondness for children confused him. He was much happier when Sheila spent time with Fred, a "stepfather" he liked. He nicknamed him "Derf" (Fred backwards). They got on. He called him "my dad." Although Sheila and Fred didn't marry until ten years later, the new "family unit" effectively moved together to a ground floor flat nearby at Frome Court. It was here that Reg Dwight was to write the songs that first made him famous.

Fred Farebrother went out of his way to support and encourage his new as-yet-unofficial stepson. The pair chatted easily about music and Fred was generous with pocket money, lifts, and morale boosts. Frome Court was a very respectable building. Here Reg got into the Beatles, and his cousin Paul Robinson has remembered the aspirant star inviting him to a Beatles Christmas show at Hammersmith Odeon. Reg

loved that the band knew the American pop and blues sounds but also wrote their own material. He was also enamored of Dusty Springfield, whose picture adorned his wall. He was now attending concerts (and football matches) regularly. He enjoyed the comedy of the Goons, Tony Hancock, and *Steptoe and Son*. He was blooming, developing, coming out of his shell. According to female schoolmates he had plenty of platonic girlfriends and was well liked for his good manners, for seeming more grown-up than his peers, and for not making unwelcome lusty passes. As his confidence blossomed, he'd boss the school's Steinway with rock and roll numbers, kicking away the piano stool and standing there hammering away like his idols. He sang too, and gladly performed at end-of-term parties and the like. A crowd would gather when he did. He was becoming something of a school star. The music teacher

The Beatles, whose blues sound Reg loved, 1963.

loathed popular music and didn't altogether approve. His history teacher said, "When you're forty, you'll either be some sort of glorified office boy or a millionaire." And at the Royal Academy the former "model pupil" began bunking off, now apparently sacrificing the spirit of Elgar for the spirit of Elvis. And evolving into the spirit of Elton.

The Northwood Hills pub, just north of Pinner, almost directly opposite Northwood Hills tube station, was large but not busy when the forward-thinking George Hill and wife Anna took tenancy in 1961. They aimed to bring some life back to its evenings by embracing the thriving new teenage crowd and putting on live music on Friday and Saturday nights. The popular pianist from their previous pub in Harrow played for a couple of weekends but then decided the traveling was excessive. Hill sought a quick replacement. That's when Fred Farebrother walked in and said his boy would love to have a go. Hill naturally assumed Farebrother was Reg's father. He

said he didn't mind taking a look at him. Fred, not content with landing the audition, drove Reg there with his "equipment"—a very basic microphone setup, which it was hoped would boost the sound of the pub's scruffy piano. Ann Hill has recalled, "He was still at school, only about fifteen. His hair was cut very short and he wore a collar and tie and grey flannel trousers. A Harris tweed sports jacket . . . kind of a gingery color. He was very shy. He told us he'd written a song called 'Come Back Baby.'"

In this faded, predominantly brown, setting, with Fred and Sheila as his roadies, Reg set up. He opened with Ray Charles's "Take These Chains." The pub patrons weren't initially blown away. According to landlord Hill, shouts of "Get off!" punctuated the hurling of crumpled crisp packets and tin ashtrays. "I think he had quite a few pints emptied into that piano as well." Yet he brazened it out, and after a few nights his "audience" seemed soothed. Eventually, they evolved to enthused clapping along. Shrewdly, young Reg didn't solely

do "modern" songs; he dropped in chestnuts like "Bye Bye Blackbird" or "Roll Out the Barrel." Some Jim Reeves. Locals who fancied themselves singers would get up for a number with him. The gypsies who'd come in took a liking to Reg and let it be known that they'd protect him against or during any random acts of violence. The atmosphere flourished. A younger clientele ventured to the pub. The area was rougher in those days, and after a drink or seven, fights would break out on weekends. Hill recalls that during one almighty fight, Reg abandoned his piano and jumped out of the window. This though was his first professional and regular gig, and he kept to it for nearly two years, saving up for better equipment. His wages were one pound and ten shillings a night plus whatever tips were brought in. Regulars simply referred to their star entertainer as "Reggie." His name may not yet have been up in lights, or indeed even anywhere outside the pub, but as Beatlemania blazed, the birth of Elton John was taking place, witnessed by happy and pugnacious drunks in Northwood Hills. (The pub is now a large Indian restaurant-cum-bar, with a slightly token-feeling plaque to Elton outside the door.)

He could feel a sea change. It was, however, a shock to his parents and his teachers when at seventeen, in early 1965, he decided to leave school, not long before he was scheduled to take his A levels (in English and music). A job offer as an office junior with the music publishing company Mills Music in Denmark Street in London's happening West End—a fiver a week for running errands and making the tea—was a dream come true for the music-obsessed youth. His trainspotter-ish knowledge of B-sides made him ideal for the gig. The grown-ups? They thought he was making a big mistake. For a start, he was the school's only A-level music student. He had four O levels, and the two As could have offered him the opportunity of university or even a full placing at the Royal Academy of Music. Helen Piena, his tutor there, thought he was squandering his talent and tried unsuccessfully to talk him round. Dad Stanley, now living in Cheshire with his new family, urged him to consider working in a bank, or the civil service, or even become an air steward. The school headmaster was, to Reg's surprise, ultimately quite understanding. "He asked me if it was really what I wanted to do," Elton recounted. "I said 'Yes,' and he said, 'All right. You have my blessing.' I was flabbergasted."

Reggie was not, at this moment, thinking of the Mills Music job as a foot in the door of pop stardom. Not remotely. Pop stars were handsome, slim, tall, glamorous, "pretty boys." They did

Denmark Street, otherwise known as "Tin Pan Alley," in the West End of London, November 1963. DJ Alan Freeman (right) in foreground, Mills Music in background.

He told us he'd written a song called 'Come Back Baby.'

ANN HILL

not have a nervous tic of pushing their glasses back up their nose every few seconds. If originally he'd donned the glasses as an affectation, a tribute to Buddy Holly, he now genuinely needed them. Yet Denmark Street was London's Tin Pan Alley, then the very center of Britain's music industry. And the offer had come to him through an unexpected route. Roy Dwight, the football-star cousin whose playing career had wound down prematurely after a bad leg injury in the 1959 FA Cup Final, and was moving into a coaching role, was also working to help young people in the sporting arena. He mentioned to Sheila that if he heard anything relevant from his impressive list of contacts which might help Reggie, he'd let her know. It turned out that a friend of a friend of Roy's, Pat Sherlock, worked for Mills Music. Roy not only set up an interview but accompanied Reggie to it. Sherlock has recalled the young man's "small hands for a piano player . . . and a funny pouting look." But Reggie was respectful and well mannered, as well as knowledgeable, so that fiver a week starting salary was put forward. He was of course thrilled. School's out forever.

Everyone who was anyone "in the business" had an office around Denmark Street; almost everyone who was a singer was dropping in regularly. In a warehouse out back, Reggie Dwight filled out order forms for sheet music, parceled goods up, took them in a wheelbarrow to the post office. His bosses were amused that he called everybody "Sir." Pat Sherlock barely noticed him, except when they had a Christmas party with a group of Chelsea FC footballers present, and Reggie was called upon to bash out some sing-along numbers on the piano. "The Old Bull and Bush" was again a helpful social tool for young Dwight. He was also spending more time with close "mate" Janet Ritchie. She was invited round to Frome Court

one night to see the new clothes he'd bought in the groovy second-hand stores around Carnaby Street. "He'd got a fur coat," she remembered. "One of the short ladies' ones all the boys were starting to wear. And a Mickey Mouse T-shirt. I'd never seen such way-out stuff before." She recalls his comment upon witnessing her surprise: "I like a bit of outrage."

Musing in 1973 over his outward flamboyance, he said, "I suppose the only regret I have about my life is that I had a bad childhood. I mean: I wasn't hit on the head every three minutes with a saucepan, but my father and mother didn't get on too well, so I didn't have too many friends or anything like that. I was very, very clammed up. I suppose I'm rebelling against that now. That's why I do all these things, because I was never allowed to go out or anything."

Well, childhood's end had now been reached and Reggie from Pinner was a West End boy. And he was soon to become a "proper" musician, playing bona fide West End gigs. At school he'd spent a few months as a pianist and occasional vocalist (doing the shoutier, Jerry Lee Lewis numbers) with local amateur band the Corvettes. Stuart Brown (guitar) and Jeff Dyson (bass) were his bandmates, knocking out rock and roll covers at youth clubs. After a short time, Dyson joined the Mockingbirds, who attained the level of supporting the Yardbirds. But then Reggie and Brown decided they wanted him back, as they were rebooting as a serious outfit under the name of Bluesology. Dyson had made useful contacts while a Mockingbird and reckoned he could get them "in" with hot Soho venues like the Marquee Club. Still fairly unfocused, they took a long while to get any traction though. "We always knew Reg was going to make it," Dyson has said. "He'd say, 'Ooh, you lot! But I'm going places . . .'" Bluesology saw themselves as being not just another beat group or rock and roll combo: they fancied incorporating jazz and blues elements in a high-class brew. Perhaps like Georgie Fame and the Blue Flames, they thought: something a little fancy. This wasn't an instant winner with teenage crowds. "We were always playing the wrong stuff, trying to appeal to minority tastes," reflected Elton years later. "Bluesology were either two months too late or three years too early."

They expanded to a quintet, adding Mick Inkpen on drums and a tenor sax player, an older guy known only as Mike. Dyson disappeared again, replaced on bass by Rex Bishop. They entered talent contests, practiced on Sundays at the Northwood Hills pub. The landlord, George Hill, ignored any hints that he could champion them as well as Reggie. "A hell of

Bluesology, 1965. L–R: Rex Bishop, Reg Dwight, Terry Patterson, Stewart Brown and, Mick Inkpen.

He'd got a fur coat. One of the short ladies' ones . . . and a Mickey Mouse T-shirt. I'd never seen such way-out stuff before.

JANET RITCHIE

a noise" was his review. So Inkpen persuaded his boss at a Bond Street jewelry manufacturer to come to a show, and Arnold Tendler was dazzled. "I was really bowled over," he told Philip Norman. "At the piano there was [this] boy in clothes even I called square. But when he played, he was marvelous. Even then he used to kick the piano stool away and even play sitting on the floor." Tendler took on the role of Bluesology's manager, providing funds for new instruments, stage clothes, and a van. Reggie, cashing in his savings from the pub gigs, finally got the electric piano he'd coveted. According to Tendler, he even had "a girlfriend, with red hair, called Gipsy."

Bluesology's new savior funded a demo, with Stuart Brown singing one side and Reggie singing his own song, "Come Back Baby," on the other. He promptly landed them the offer of a recording contract with the Fontana label. OK, maybe the labels were tossing out record deals liberally in the giddy new gold rush of that post-Beatlemania era, and the contract was ludicrously one-sided, but Reggie and Bluesology were understandably exultant. Not only was "Come Back Baby" the A-side, but Mills Music, his day job employers, picked up their proud office boy's publishing. The single was released in July 1965, bang in the middle of the summer of the Rolling Stones' "Satisfaction," the Byrds' "Mr. Tambourine Man," and the Animals' "We Gotta Get out of This Place." And that's when reality bit. It sank without trace, but not before Reggie had experienced the thrill of hearing its brisk if basic charms on Radio Luxembourg. Still, he was now a pro. He was a recording artist. He'd made a debut record, which he'd written and sung. He was going places.

2

THE CAPTAIN & THE KID, STEPPING IN THE RING

"We were complete opposites—town mouse and country mouse. But the one thing we had in common was being mad about pop music. And both being desperate to write songs.

BERNIE TAUPIN

Mention Bluesology to any fan of Elton John and most will know that he was a member. They'll know that in 1966, Bluesology became Long John Baldry's backing band. Sixties buffs will cite that their agency booked them out as a live session band for visiting American acts, from the Isley Brothers to Major Lance to Patti LaBelle. Experts will know they recorded with one of Elton's heroes, Little Richard, at Abbey Road. Yet perhaps the moment Bluesology most significantly impacted young Reg Dwight's career was when he chose a new solo stage name by borrowing those of two band members: saxophonist Elton Dean and singer Mr. Baldry. Thus was Elton John, the character, the alter ego, the superstar, born.

Enjoying the liberated buzz of the decade, Reggie was working for Mills Music by day and dividing his nights between Bluesology gigs and solo pub dates. As Bluesology gradually blossomed, it was evident to most clued-up observers that he was the heartbeat, the true talent in the effective and adaptable ensemble. His mother and step-dad were still keenly supportive. Manager Tendler put the band in matching outfits. "Reg looked awful, though I don't think any of us looked wonderful," early drummer Mick Inkpen has recalled. Stewart Brown was the heartthrob, the one the girls flocked towards. When "Come Back Baby" failed to catch the popular imagination, Reg openly admitted to his bandmates that lyric writing wasn't his forte. The other side, sung by Brown, was a Jimmy Witherspoon cover. Publicity shots showed the band posing stiltedly outside the Tower of London, Reggie already instantly recognizable from the rest with his conservative haircut and dark-rimmed specs.

PREVIOUS PAGE: Reg Dwight with lyricist Bernie Taupin shortly after they signed contracts with Dick James Music, London, 1968.
LEFT: Bluesology gave live support to Patti LaBelle and the Bluebelles on their UK tour, 1966.

After a successful talent show at the Kilburn State, the Roy Tempest Agency offered Bluesology regular gigs as backing musicians. They embarked now on three years of hard work, slogging away as musicians on demand, hired hands for touring acts, often throwing in a set as the support band. Tempest's entrepreneurial skills were unorthodox: on the cheap, he'd bring over to the UK bands who were on the slide in America. His notion was that he and they could milk a good fortnight of shows here, sometimes squeezing in two a night if the profit margins appealed to him. Wilson Pickett arrived expecting top-of-the-range session men, and his musical director flew over, listened to Bluesology's best efforts, and said no. They added experience, in the form of trumpeter Pat Higgs and tenor saxophonist Dave Murphy. Higgs was capable of writing out arrangements in advance, a new level for the younger lads. When Major Lance, known for his articulate Curtis Mayfield–penned hit "Um, Um, Um, Um, Um, Um" came over, they felt more confident. One night at the Q Club, Mick Jagger, Keith Richards, and Alexis Korner were in attendance. For the pianist from Pinner, this was all extremely exciting. Exhausting, sure,

and lugging all that gear around without roadies was a grind, but he'd stepped up from staring at record labels in his bedroom to being personally involved in the dream factory.

Bluesology toured and played with Patti LaBelle and the Bluebells (one of whom was Cindy Birdsong, a Supreme to be), the Drifters, Doris Troy (including a gig at the Cavern in Liverpool), and veteran crooners the Inkspots. If Reggie was bursting to express his personality, he kept it well restrained for now. He was just one of the guys, who liked talking about music almost as much as playing it. Other members have said he wasn't a big one for after-show party shenanigans, bar tossing in a few *Goon Show* and Morecambe and Wise gags. A second single, "Mr. Frantic," was released in 1966. Stewart Brown sang the B-side, a cover of B. B. King's "Every Day I Have the Blues," but again a Reggie original composition was chosen as the A-side. "Mr. Frantic" was scarcely more innovative than "Come Back Baby," the lyrics conventional platitudes, but its faint Motown-soul influences gave it a touch more spark. Accordingly, it crept to the dizzying chart heights of "about number 150," in the estimation of drummer Inkpen.

They now had a reputation as reliable and diligent, and the tours with others were giving Dwight insight into the work and showmanship required to make it on the live circuit. It was going well enough—his Bluesology wages were pushing £20 a week—for him to amicably give his notice at Mills Music. Tiring of Tempest's whip-cracking, the band left him and hooked up with Marquee Enterprises, which promised gigs at Soho's where-the-action-was Marquee Club. They supported the Who, Manfred Mann, and others, with celebrities in the audience. This was a great shop window, they figured. At the same time they'd watch bands like those of Spencer Davis or Georgie Fame and realize they had a lot of ground to make up. Ambitious Elton later reflected on the experience as being mundane and mediocre. He envied the Move, having seen them make it big. He wanted some of that.

They fulfilled a tough tour of their own in Europe, playing four hours a night in Hamburg for a month. But like the Beatles, they earned their spurs there. They could play a bit now. Fatigue was also a factor, however. There were personnel changes, with just Reg and Stewart of the original members surviving the cull. Saxophonist David Murphy stayed, joined by bassist Fred Gandy, drummer Paul Gale, and trumpeter Chris Bateson. And then came the entrance of Long John Baldry. Let the hope and the heartaches begin.

Some say Baldry was the man who discovered Elton John. There's an argument for that, but also a case for saying he didn't spot the superstar under his nose. Baldry's presence and talent commanded great respect, which Elton always retained for him. The six-foot-seven Baldry saw the band playing in Kensington (opposite the Victoria and Albert Museum) and offered them a job. This was a seal of approval from a man who was already approaching legendary status. He'd pioneered blues singing in the UK, and had performed with Alexis Korner's Blues Incorporated, who'd inspired the Stones, Led Zeppelin, Rod Stewart (another youngster he'd encouraged), and Cream. He had kudos and contacts. Not to mention a beautiful, resonant singing voice.

So Bluesology and Baldry became an item for the next two years. They grew into a shape-shifting, flexible entity, with members such as Marsha Hunt (soon to be the star of *Hair*),

I think that's the graveyard of musicians, playing cabaret. I'd rather be dead than work in cabaret.

ELTON JOHN

guitarist Neil Hubbard (later a key element of Bryan Ferry and Roxy Music's sound), and the aforementioned Elton Dean bolstering the numbers. Dean, who went on to play with Soft Machine and Keith Tippett, has remembered Dwight as "a frustrated singer." In this modified incarnation of Bluesology, he was way down the queue when it came to vocalists. At rehearsals, he'd offer up songs he'd written, to little avail. There was another Bluesology single, "Since I Found You Baby," but it was sung by Stewart Brown and written by, believe it or not, popular television light entertainer and actor Kenny Lynch. By early '67, Baldry was growing frustrated that Bluesology were not matching the momentum of his previous outfit Steampacket, and decided to move towards more mainstream balladry. And before the year was out, he'd hit No. 1 with the epic yearning torch song "Let the Heartaches Begin," written by Tony Macaulay and John Macleod. Baldry (nicknamed Sugarbear) nonetheless was later to play a key part in cheering up his erstwhile pianist, as lyrically documented in the 1975 hit "Someone Saved My Life Tonight."

Reg, grumpy, now pouted a little. "I think that's the graveyard of musicians, playing cabaret," the twenty-year-old huffed to *Rolling Stone*'s Paul Gambaccini in 1973. "I'd rather be dead than work in cabaret." He bade farewell to Bluesology later that same year, as did Brown and Dean. One Caleb Quaye joined as a replacement, not knowing at this stage that he'd later be a regular member of Elton John's band, but the ensemble wound up in '68. As for Reggie, he'd seen an ad in the *New Musical Express* which tickled his fancy. It was to lead to the most significant meeting of his career, and one which changed his life immeasurably.

On June 17, 1967, the *NME*—once the cool cat of the music press—ran the following ad:

LIBERTY WANTS TALENT.
ARTISTES/COMPOSERS/SINGER-MUSICIANS.
Call or write Ray Williams.

Williams, who was launching Liberty Records, was himself a cool cat on the London music scene of the day. Still a teenager, he'd already worked in PR for the likes of the Kinks, the Hollies, and Sonny & Cher, and been involved with the very essence of Swinging Sixties London: TV pop show *Ready Steady Go!* Presenter Cathy McGowan had picked him as her assistant, not least because he was famously handsome, blond, and dashing. He'd often modeled for *Mod's Monthly* magazine. Liberty, a US label, had been part of EMI but was now going independent, and had appointed the finger-on-the-pulse Williams as head of A&R.

And you needed a finger-on-the-pulse kind of guy. That year had seen radical changes in the temperature, tone, and timbre of British pop. Things were shifting apace in the counterculture, in the underground, in fashion and the arts. The Beatles had put out the epochal *Sgt. Pepper's Lonely Hearts Club Band.* Pink Floyd and others were wowing the "alternative" youth with psychedelia. Bob Dylan—and, closer to home, Keith Reid's lyrics for Procol Harum's "A Whiter Shade of Pale"—were promoting more imaginative, challenging use of words in pop songs.

Reg Dwight wrote in reply to the ad, disgruntled before a gig in Newcastle with Bluesology. Ray Williams invited him to his office in Mayfair's Albemarle Street for a chat. Reg's prime motivation was that he was tiring of life on the road with Baldry's band. Years later, he related to Paul Gambaccini, "I told him I couldn't write lyrics and I couldn't sing very well, but I thought I could write songs." Williams got him to audition in a studio: rather uninspiringly, Dwight did five Jim Reeves and Ray Charles songs. He was told, effectively, not to call us, we'll call you.

Pianists were not exactly in vogue as guitar bands surged to glory. Reg was anything but hip, especially when viewed by a man who was the walking epitome of contemporaneous cool. However, Williams wasn't completely unimpressed. He could see the degree to which Dwight metamorphosed into another character while singing. He did helpfully suggest that after he'd made some decent demos he should try Dick James, the Beatles' music publisher. And he helped him make those demos, in the familiar environs of Denmark Street. This wasn't Williams's only useful input. He'd had another interviewee who not only couldn't sing, but couldn't play, but pitched himself as a poet whose lyrics might work with the music of others. The A&R man, not for a moment imagining he was performing one of

Dick James and
Brian Epstein, 1964.

music history's most impactful matchmaking ceremonies, advised Reggie to consider getting in touch with him. Williams handed over an envelope containing some pages of lyrics he'd been sent, with a letter, from Lincolnshire. The singer opened the envelope on the tube home. Enter, thus, Bernie Taupin.

While Williams moved his attention to acts he felt were worth signing—the Bonzo Dog Doo-Dah Band, Jeff Lynne (later of the Move and ELO), and Mike Batt (later of the Wombles and much besides)—Reggie was left staring at a wad of lyrics with peculiar titles like "Year of the Teddy Bear" and "Sad-Eyed Queen of Laughing Lake." Yet Williams was quietly still pulling for Dwight, on some level perhaps because he felt sorry for him, having perceived a talented but not content young man. Liberty weren't interested, but he introduced Dwight to writers and musicians in Dick James's orbit.

James had been in the right place at the right time to land a lucky meeting with Brian Epstein and grab the incomparably fruitful Lennon-McCartney publishing. He'd showed savvy in setting up Northern Songs, which generously split royalties 50–50 with the writers, thus earning their trust. The radical move dropped a bomb on the way things had always been done in Tin Pan Alley. For all this, he was well liked by all in the business and stayed ahead of the curve without arousing antipathy. Every aspiring songwriter now begged an audience with him, and soon DJM (Dick James Music) was a huge, thriving operation, with Dick's son Stephen involved from an early age. It was he who advocated an in-house recording studio, and it was there that Reggie worked with young writers Nicky James and Kirk Duncan through the summer of '67. They brought in Tony Murray (later of the Troggs) on bass and Dave Hinds on drums.

He'd got something special . . . every day, a little bit more would come out.

CALEB QUAYE

They recorded Dwight-James-Duncan collaborations, which were offered to the Hollies or other ranking bands. Reggie sang, but reports suggest his confidence was low and that he saw his vocals as just a guide, a place-holder. The studio engineer was his old friend/rival Caleb Quaye, who liked to pull his leg, and that may in context have clipped his wings, his freedom to be someone other than a kid from Pinner. As things settled in, however, Quaye was more respectful, singing Dwight's praises. "He'd got something special . . . every day, a little bit more of it would come out." Reggie enjoyed encountering the big names who'd come by: Graham Nash, then with the Hollies, was helpful beyond the call of duty. After they'd clocked off, he and bandmate Allan Clarke would take the young hopefuls out for excessive drinks.

Meanwhile, seventeen-year-old Bernie Taupin had found his way to London, naively optimistic, expecting the streets to be paved with gold. He lodged with his uncle in Putney, perhaps assuming he'd soon have enough to get his own place. As he entered Liberty Records, he, too, saw Graham Nash on the steps and felt beyond doubt that he had hit the big time. Ray Williams put together a meeting between Taupin and Dwight at Dick James Music. A diffident Taupin was even more gauchely dressed than Reggie. At DJM he waited nervously in the control room, observing Reggie finishing a piano part. Caleb Quaye inquired who he was and if he was meant to be there. When Reggie came out and asked if Bernie was "the lyricist," the pair popped out for a coffee and chat in a Tottenham Court Road café.

Their shared love of music made for an easy initial level of bonding. Both, like most young people then, loved the Beatles, Dylan, Motown. Both struck each other as disarmingly humble. Both were trainspotters when it came to favorite records and bands. And yet they realized that they'd had completely contrasting upbringings: happy versus troubled, a farm versus suburbia, a warm, loving father versus a remote, distant one.

Elton playing on the road in blues clubs versus Bernie mucking out stables. Taupin has said, "We were complete opposites—town mouse and country mouse. But the one thing we had in common was being mad about pop music. And both being desperate to write songs." By the second cup of coffee, they'd committed to giving it a go. Reggie introduced Bernie to Nicky James and Kirk Duncan, who flicked through Bernie's pages of lyrics and seemed enthused. They weren't "possessive" about their colleague. And soon Dwight and Taupin became the default writing pair. The team soon crafted their first Taupin co-write, "Scarecrow." Bernie was exhilarated to show the acetate to his uncle, but it had no afterlife. Momentum gathered though, and a prolific, motivated Bernie would post lyrics to Reggie. When at DJM, Bernie would hand over his sheets of paper and Reggie would depart to the piano in another room, shyly not wanting to be watched while he composed. He was quick. In usually around ten minutes he'd be back with a melody and chord structure. Quaye and DJM were supportive and accommodating, allowing sessions to run late into the night. For Reggie, this was ideal—his weak spot of lyric writing was being taken care of. It was ideal for Bernie too—he felt Reggie found the right tone each time and never, or rarely, edited or quibbled about long or incongruous words. The happening summer of '67 wasn't theirs, but they were laying foundations for the longer game.

Sleaford, a market town in Lincolnshire, hasn't delivered as many famous people as Pinner. Its list is almost apologetic—the novelist Thomas Shipman, the actor Joseph Smedley, the actor-comedian Jennifer Saunders. Eric Thompson, who narrated *The Magic Roundabout*. Contemporary electro-punks Sleaford Mods aren't from there, but from nearby Grantham. But Bernie Taupin was born there and grew up on a farm. As "Goodbye Yellow Brick Road" states, there were times during the early, pre-success days in London when he wished he'd listened to his old man and stayed there.

He was born on May 22, 1950 at Flatters farmhouse, between Sleaford and the village of Anwick. It had no electricity. His roots were French, Burgundy-based: his grandfather moved to London. His father, Robert Taupin, was educated in Dijon and his mother, Daphne, in Switzerland. The daughter of a classics teacher whose influence fed Bernie's love of words, she studied French literature and Russian, becoming a fluent French speaker, working as a nanny. The couple met in London, marrying in 1947.

Dropping out from studies as a lawyer, with health issues, Bernie's dad found employment as a stockman on a large

Reg Dwight and Bernie Taupin, London, 1967.

farm near Market Rasen. They eventually moved to Rowston Manor, which did have electricity. When Robert decided to go independent as a farmer, the family took on the dilapidated estate Maltkiln Farm, in Owmby-by-Spital. Bernie's brother Kit, eleven years his junior, was born there. It was from there that Bernie sent his hopeful letter to Liberty.

He'd grown up inspired by his grandfather's recitations of Tennyson and Coleridge, by *Winnie-the-Pooh*, by *The Wind in the Willows*, by C. S. Lewis's Narnia tales, and by Roman Catholicism (he'd been an altar boy at the local church). He grew into Wild West stories, engrossed in books and films about Billy the Kid, Jesse James, Wyatt Earp, Davy Crockett. He became, inevitably, a writer. By the age of ten he was scribbling his own stories about American cowboys: a symbol or metaphor which he would return to repeatedly. The uncle in Putney who

was to put him up when he came to meet Reggie turned him on to music: Woody Guthrie, Lonnie Donegan, Leadbelly. He was fascinated by the perceived grit and glamour of all things American. Owmby-by-Spital wasn't on the cutting edge of new music, but gradually, through Radio Luxembourg, Bernie absorbed rock and roll and country, with a leaning towards the latter. Johnny Cash seemed like another cowboy to him. He tried to toughen up as a teen, puttng aside literature and trying to dress to fit in with other youths, professing fondness for Jerry Lee Lewis or Little Richard. Yet when he heard Bob Dylan singing "The Times They Are a-Changin'" on the radio, his visceral reaction to words blazed again. "The voice was like broken glass, like spitting. The words were like arrows being shot straight into the heart of the establishment. That made me realize what the words of a song could do."

We always believed in Reg, and thought he had talent. But the main thing was, we just liked him.

STEPHEN JAMES

He hoped to use his words as a reporter on the *Lincolnshire Standard*, but was given an apprenticeship in the print room. Such a steady job wasn't to be sniffed at, yet Bernie did. He began his bad-boy period. Bored and taking to drink, he swore at the foreman and packed it in. He sulked and skulked around at home, his parents disappointed. He'd pen pages of lyrics in his bedroom, but the pop world seemed, and was, a long way away. "I was so far from the center of everything. I had no idea how record companies or songwriters worked." At the start of 1967, the year he met Elton John, he was laboring on a chicken farm, at one stage carrying hundreds of chicken corpses to the incinerator after an outbreak of fowl pest.

Upon seeing the *New Musical Express* ad, he typed out some lyrics, intending to send them to Ray Williams. Or at least daydreaming about doing that. He never actually sent them. In an implausibly lucky break, his mother, finding the envelope doing not very much on the mantelpiece, posted it.

Now, with Taupin and Dwight starting to build more tangible dreams by writing together in London, there came a boost. Stephen James decided their demos were promising. To the pair's surprise they were called in for a meeting with Dick. He in turn warmed to their polite shyness and Reggie's flashes of wit. Stephen has said, "We always believed in Reg, and thought he had talent. But the main thing was, we just liked him." Dick James contracted Dwight and Taupin as songwriters. They were thrilled. For Dwight, it meant he could finally quit slogging away with Bluesology. For Taupin, it was just a surreal fantasy come true. "To actually be given money

for writing songs! I couldn't believe they were serious." One person who didn't love this arrangement was Ray Williams, without whom the duo would never have met. He got nothing from the deal, but given that he was involved with A-list movers and shakers, swiftly got over it. Stephen James, like so many not rating Reg as a potential pop star, saw the pair solely as writers, nudging them to study recent hits by female stars like Lulu, Sandie Shaw, and Dusty Springfield and try to mimic those. They formally signed with DJM on November 7. (Reggie's mother and Bernie's father served as witnesses). They were given a modest advance of £100 and even more modest weekly retainers (set against future royalties).

Over the next two years they would indeed write for Lulu, as well as Roger Cook and others, though the yellow-brick road was still short of being paved with gold. "It was like two years of misery, writing garbage," the singer later moaned. Initially, as Stephen touted their songs around A&R departments, response was healthy but not heated. Stephen noticed that experienced hands were telling him that the songs were too quirky for established artists but that the singer was interesting, different. So the James family again proved they never missed

LEFT: Reg Dwight and Bernie Taupin, London, 1967.
RIGHT: Lulu, 1967, one of the new songwriting duo's early artists.

a trick, as Stephen offered Reggie a recording deal. Again, Reggie was delighted, even though the deal was tiny (and akin to the one he'd had with Bluesology). Reinvigorated, he made a concerted attempt to lose weight. He succeeded, to a degree, with some at the time even describing him as "gaunt." His last effort to get more vocal slots in Bluesology had collapsed when Long John Baldry got his chart-topping hit, which meant there was no way he'd be sharing the limelight with another singer. Loathing the cabaret circuit, Reg packed his bags and ran away to his own circus.

Flying back to London after a Bluesology gig in Edinburgh in December, he asked the other musicians to help him come up with his solo artist name. Even Reg Dwight was aware that Reg Dwight was not a ticket-selling, up-in-lights moniker. On the plane, he even asked saxophonist Elton Dean outright if he could steal his name. "That's a bit strong, Reg," muttered Dean.

According to Dean, Reg went away and came back a minute later. "OK," he said, "is it all right if I call myself Elton John?" He'd scanned the heads in the seats including Baldry's, trying out the various permutations. Neither of the nominees objected. And so Reggie Dwight was no more. Long—he hoped—live Elton John. As 1967 became 1968, he celebrated his new persona by acquiring a girlfriend. Not only that, she became his fiancée.

They met on Christmas Eve. Reg, who from now on we'll call Elton, was playing one of his final Bluesology gigs in Sheffield. Linda Woodrow was experiencing alleged abuse from her then-boyfriend, and Elton made an unlikely gallant white knight, rescuing her from his unpleasantness. That was Elton's version anyway. According to David Buckley's biography Linda stated that this was not a boyfriend, just her companion on the fateful night. She reckoned she and Elton had a chemistry instantly—"we clicked straight away. . . . I found him funny and enjoyed his

Elton's first
publicity pictures,
Hampstead,
London, January
1968.

company." He invited her to subsequent gigs, and for the next six months they were, to all intents and purposes, dating. They had long phone calls between Sheffield and London, and soon Linda felt confident enough in Elton's affections to move down to London. Elton, declaring himself in love, finally moved out of his mother and step-dad's Frome Court maisonette: goodbye, Pinner. Or, as it transpires, so long for now. He moved in to a flat the competent and can-do Linda had found in Islington's Furlong Road. Bernie, having joined his writing partner in Pinner for a while, now tagged along. Linda was to later tell a newspaper that "where Elton went, he did," and that neither paid any rent. She stumped up for all the bills, she said. "I didn't mind—I was in love and wanted to be with him."

Linda, two years older than her twenty-one-year-old beau, had on paper a great deal more money than the starving artists. An upper-middle-class graduate of a finishing school, she was the heiress to Epicure Products, an American pickled onion giant. Her inheritance was in a trust fund, however, so she worked for the time being as a secretary. When she and Elton got engaged, she later told the *Hamilton Spectator*, she paid for her own £200 engagement ring. Invitations were posted for a June 1968 wedding.

Elton, though, was getting frosty feet. Partly in denial, he was unhappy about his still-struggling music career, a feeling only stoked by his witnessing the successes of friends. Neither Bernie nor Elton's mother, Sheila, were enthused by the engagement. Linda was sensible, practical, and envisaged her fiancé sidelining the stalling music and getting a proper job with a solid income as a path to future parenthood. Within Elton's psyche, this not only echoed his father's value system but felt like a slight to the potential of the stronger songs he and Bernie were now creating. She wasn't, Elton has hinted, a great pop music fan.

Of course, with hindsight, there were other major fault lines. Linda has recalled that physical intimacy was infrequent. At the time, inexperienced herself, she assumed that was just how things went. Later in life she understood matters differently. Used to living with his parents, he—and Bernie—found domestic life challenging. Linda wanted order, normality. The songwriters found her strict, especially for the times. Bernie's request to put a poster of Simon and Garfunkel on his wall was turned down. He disliked her dog, who regularly emptied his bowels on the doorstep. Yet much of this is partisan criticism after the event. On one level, the couple were fond of the fresh spin they put on each other's perspective, and Elton was at first caught up in a rush of novel feelings. Until he wasn't. Linda thought his angst was about his music. His friends, or some of them, knew otherwise. Long John Baldry's views were to prove particularly influential.

LEFT: Chaneling Jerry Lee Lewis during a live show, 1968.
TOP RIGHT: In 1968, shortly after signing his contract with Dick James Music.

3

"THE NEW MESSIAH IS HERE"

"I was sort of pushed into being a singer because nobody recorded our songs. Once I got a taste of being a performer, I really liked it."

ELTON JOHN

Elton's muddled and botched engagement was stirring turmoil in his soul. So much so that he (kind of) attempted suicide, although bathos rather than pathos resulted. Bernie came out of his bedroom in Linda's Islington place one night, smelling gas. He found Elton with his head in the oven, the rest of his body prone on the kitchen floor. Elton had taken the wise precaution of leaving the windows open and had even placed a comfortable pillow for his head inside the stove. In truth it seems less a grandiose statement, more a highly flawed, attention-seeking practice run. In 2018, Bernie reiterated the tale to *CBS Sunday Morning* interviewer Lee Cowan, adding of the subsequent lyrics to "Someone Saved My Life Tonight" that "I wrote it from his point of view. It was a very . . . comical incident, of him being depressed and making an attempt—a very feeble attempt, I might add—at suicide. Leaving the windows open when the oven was on. And me coming in and going, 'What are you doing? Get off the floor! This is silly. Don't be a silly boy!' But it was a serious cry for help, so it made a good ingredient for a song. It's still a great song to this day."

At the root of this tragedy-farce crossover, however, lies a seriousness. Elton, clearly, could not marry Linda. A few weeks later he and Bernie were out drinking near Carnaby Street, at the pop star hang-out the Bag O'Nails, with Long John Baldry. They were all plastered. Baldry bit the bullet and called it like he saw it. He told Elton to stop being ridiculous, to admit that he didn't love Linda, and that he should stop hand-wringing and procrastinating and end it now for both their sakes. Elton hadn't even realized that Baldry was gay, and still wasn't sure if he himself was, though Baldry had seen it. "If you marry this woman you'll destroy two lives—yours and hers." Years on, Elton admitted this insight "saved his life," and Bernie captured the story in the lyrics to the epic "Someone Saved My Life Tonight." The songwriting pair staggered home in the early hours and, allowing the drink to speak, Elton broke the news of his epiphany to Linda. For all the previous signs and clues, she was stunned, hurt, and not a little heartbroken. Her ex-fiancé, however, felt a wave of relief, like an aching tooth had been pulled. That same day, Fred, his stepfather, came over to help him pack and move back to Pinner. Bernie joined them within a week. Poignantly, Linda and Elton have never spoken to each other again.

As if to emphasize a new chapter in his life—and though it may not have seemed so at first, success wasn't too far away now—Elton was trying to sharpen up his image, wearing clothes

PREVIOUS PAGE: Playing a black grand piano, November, 1970.
ABOVE: Posing for a portrait, London, 1969.

that avoided hippy clichés but exuded bright colors and flirted, tentatively at first, with outrageousness. Bernie's lyrics were going through a phase of sixties-soaked acid lingo, and when Elton's debut single emerged on Philips on March 1, 1968, it was the singer's own composition (though he magnanimously shared credit with his now closest friend). "I've Been Loving You," produced by Caleb Quaye, was not a classic, but it can lay claim to getting him his first sniffs of press. As a tangent, he and Taupin had a song accepted as a contender for the UK's entry for the 1969 Eurovision Song Contest, back then considered rather less of an artistic accolade than it would become. Lulu sang "I Can't Go on Living Without You" It came sixth out of six of her

shortlist, but the nation's winner, "Boom Bang-a-Bang," went on to tie for top place in the final contest. Elton later expressed relief that his song had tanked, imagining the path his career might have taken had the effort taken off. He took credit/blame for the lyrics again, dismissing them in what's commonly described as "strong language." At least his mum had voted for his song, as mums do. Many times.

He crafted away, producing enough demos for an album that never saw the light of day. He sidelined as a session pianist, featuring on tracks by the Hollies (piano on "He Ain't Heavy, He's My Brother"), the Scaffold (backing vocals on "Lily the Pink," a Christmas No. 1), and on such unforgettable classics as the Barron Knights' "An Olympic Record." While recording that one at Abbey Road, he was overjoyed to bump into Paul McCartney, who sat at the piano and showed Bernie and him something he'd just written. It was "Hey Jude." This probably only added to Elton's frustration that the hackneyed formulaic songs he was writing for others were to the taste of neither himself nor their intended interpreters, and might explain the ghastly title of a track on his debut album—"Hay Chewed." Yet this thwarted ambition gave him a shove towards taking on the role of solo performer more committedly. According to David Buckley's biography of Elton, he said, "I was sort of pushed into being a singer because nobody recorded our songs. Once I got a taste of being a performer, I really liked it."

There was help and encouragement from Steve Brown, a promo man at DJM, who contradicted Dick James and said John and Taupin should focus on their own material. He advised them to write what they felt. Lionel Conway in the publishing department also assisted, getting the pair's song "Taking the Sun from My Eyes" on a B-side by TV star Ayshea Brough and their composition "The Tide Will Turn for Rebecca" recorded by actor Edward Woodward. Experienced songwriting team Roger Cook and Roger Greenaway also boosted their morale, with Cook himself recording their song "Skyline Pigeon." Another Elton John single came out, with "Lady Samantha" a vast improvement on its predecessor. Caleb Quaye's guitar was again an attractive factor, and the chorus showed the duo were beginning to master the tropes of their trade. Elton's voice, too, was more confident, more itself (and didn't fall back on the Americanisms he'd later adopt as a habit). It seemed a blessing in disguise that he'd failed the auditions he'd recently taken with prog giants King Crimson and Gentle Giant. Released in January 1969, the single failed to chart but gathered plenty of radio play. It boded well for the year ahead. The industry knew who Elton John was now, and Dick James became a convert to

LEFT: In flamboyant bow-tie and shirt, London, 1969.

empty sky / elton john

EMPTY SKY

TRACK LIST

SIDE ONE
Empty Sky
Val-Hala
Western Ford Gateway
Hymn 2000

SIDE TWO
Lady What's Tomorrow
Sails
The Scaffold
Skyline Pigeon
Gulliver/Hay Chewed/Reprise

Recorded at Dick James Music Studios, London, England
Produced by Steve Brown
Released June 6, 1969 (UK), January 13, 1975 (US)
Label DJM Records, DJLPS 403
Highest chart position on release US 6

PERSONNEL

Elton John: vocals, piano, organ, Fender Rhodes, harpsichord
Caleb Quaye: electric guitar, acoustic guitar, congas
Tony Murray: bass guitar
Roger Pope: drums, percussion
Nigel Olsson: drums on "Lady What's Tomorrow"
Don Fay: saxophone, flute
Graham Vickery: harmonica

COVER ART

Dave Larkham: sleeve design, illustration

NOTES

"Val-Hala" was properly titled "Valhalla" on the 1975 US reissue. "Hay Chewed" was mistakenly titled "It's Hay-Chewed" on the 1995 CD reissue.

his charge being a singer as well as a writer. There was even a John Peel session.

Steve Brown had produced the single, and was given the reins of the Elton John debut album. He swiftly got the team recording "It's Me That You Need" as the next single, complete with orchestra, released on Dick's own label DJM. The budget was limited, so album sessions took place through the early months of 1969 on the 8-track downstairs at DJM. *Empty Sky* revealed its new horizons on June 6 in the UK, though it wasn't released in the States until six years later, by when he was a huge name and it rose to No. 6 there. Elton has since told *Spectacle*, "I wasn't sure what sound I was going for—maybe Leonard Cohen," but it's much rockier and busier than that suggests. The excited and excitable eight-minute title track, the opener, has something of the sixties' flavor of rhythm meeting euphoria, perhaps akin to the giddy richness of Donovan's "Barabajagal" or a slightly more relaxed the Who. "Val-Hala" was an early indication of the writers' knack for melancholy, tempered moods. Elton dabbled on the harpsichord on a few numbers, while Caleb played guitars and the rhythm section consisted of Tony Murray and Roger Pope. Nigel Olsson, then of the Spencer Davis Group, handled drums on "Lady What's Tomorrow?" He and then-bandmate bassist Dee Murray would soon join the "classic" early seventies Elton John band. "Skyline Pigeon," which is Elton playing solo, is probably the album's most popularly loved song, having since become a relatively frequent feature in live shows. The album finale, "Gulliver/ Hay Chewed/Reprise," is a bizarre Frankenstein's monster of a closing song followed by brief excerpts of every track, which presumably seemed like a wild psychedelic idea at the time. Hey, it was still, just, the sixties.

Elton has with hindsight described the album as naïve, but to those only familiar with his later, slicker, smooth-edged work it's refreshingly robust, sounding more spiritually akin to some of the rock bands of the day than singer-songwriter sweetness. Vocally, he lets it all hang out, going somewhat crazy over the epic title cut's outro. He remembers the recording sessions fondly, and has recalled walking "home" at four in the morning to his lodgings in Oxford Street, at the Salvation Army HQ (conveniently run by Steve Brown's father). When they finished it, he had the rush of feeling that the title track "floored" him. "I thought it was the best thing I'd ever heard in my life," he said in the liner notes to a nineties reissue. Of the original release, BBC DJ David Symonds wrote, "Elton John plays and pleases

on this album but does not confine himself to the brighter side of life." The *Evening Standard* called it "nicely recorded, but unadventurous" and while praising the "sweet" music, looked down its nose at Bernie's lyrics, deeming them "self-consciously cultured and 'poetic.'" It then conceded that, "To be fair . . . he has talent."

"Skyline Pigeon" had already had a Roger Cook rendition (under the name Roger James Cooke), and was also soon to be covered by Guy Darrell, his band Deep Feeling, Dana, Judith Durham (of the Seekers), and the great Gene Pitney. Elton himself re-recorded it with his band—and a Paul Buckmaster string arrangement—three years later, and that version showed up on the B-side of "Daniel." Received wisdom has it that *Empty Sky*, which at first sold fewer than four thousand copies, is not without charm but flounders around looking for its singer's own style or voice. There's some truth in the reservation, and there are spells where it's plainly mimicking the Beatles or Traffic, but to 2019 ears it reveals a surprisingly gutsy, gritty Elton.

He was generally in demand now. He took paid jobs to sing cover versions of hits, popular at the time, for the *Top of the Pops* series of budget albums (which, after a branding oversight by the BBC, weren't actually owned by the TV show). He perfected his imitation game, tackling everything from Mungo Jerry's "In the Summertime" to Stevie Wonder's "Signed, Sealed, Delivered I'm Yours" to Cat Stevens's "Lady D'Arbanville" to—a difficult, high one, he confessed—Robin Gibb's "Saved by the Bell." He also landed work as a backing vocalist, and has claimed he's on the England 1970 World Cup Squad's "Back

LEFT: Elton with his band members Dee Murray (left) and Nigel Olsson (center), 1969.
RIGHT: With Bernie Taupin, London, 1969.

I thought [*Empty Sky*] was the best thing I'd ever heard in my life.

ELTON JOHN

Home" as well as Tom Jones's "Daughter of Darkness." He played piano on Roger "Supertramp" Hodgson's debut single (which emerged under the name Argosy). He moonlighted with the Bread and Beer Band alongside Caleb Quaye, Roger Pope, and the Hollies' Bernie Calvert. Their self-titled Abbey Road album was produced by a young Chris Thomas, much later to helm Elton's own work, but after a single bombed this album was nixed.

As if this wasn't enough (to, perhaps, take his mind off his false start in his love life), Elton worked occasional shifts in a Soho record shop. At Music Land in Berwick Street he'd serve others while enjoying extra listens to favorites like Joni Mitchell, Jimi Hendrix, Bob Dylan, and Blood, Sweat and Tears. When Bob Harris, not yet known as "DJ Whispering Bob" but an editor at *Time Out*, came in to the shop, Elton agreed to stock copies of Bob's magazine if he would review *Empty Sky.*

OK, he may have been still living with Sheila and "Derf" (and Bernie) and some goldfish, but gradually now things were coming along. Three Dog Night called him—in Pinner—to inform him they were recording "Lady Samantha." The rocker in him loved that. Significantly, in October his diary recorded that he wrote "Your Song." By the spring of the next year, when his self-titled second album came out, *Melody Maker* was writing, "Is this the year of Elton John?"

And it was. The seventies became him, and he was among those who became the seventies. With hindsight, it's bizarre to realize he began that decade still kipping in a bunk bed at his mum's in Pinner—as was Bernie. The pair would still hang around DJM's offices, hoping for a bigger break. Tiny ones came: Elton even appeared on *Top of the Pops* twice, in the background, singing backing vocals for Brotherhood of Man's "United We

Stand" and with Pickettywitch. He'd played piano onstage with Simon Dupree and the Big Sound (of "Kites" fame) and DJM organized some small-scale live shows under his own name. Yet when they green-lit the sessions for a second album, they were covertly thinking of it as a last chance for an artist they'd already spent more money on trying to break than they'd envisaged.

They gave it every chance. Steve Brown persuaded Dick James to fund recordings at Trident Studios in Soho. He even tried to get George Martin, the Beatles' legendary producer, on board, but Martin, understandably given his CV, wanted to be in charge of both production and arrangements. Brown had already booked Paul Buckmaster for the latter. So ultimately responsibilities were split between Buckmaster and producer Gus Dudgeon. Dudgeon was a graduate of West Hampstead's Decca Studios who'd worked with the Zombies, John Mayall, Ten Years After, and Michael Chapman, thus learning how to dress both rock dynamics and singer-songwriter subtlety. With Buckmaster, he'd added color to David Bowie's "Space Oddity," and his work with the Bonzo Dog Doo-Dah Band was fashionable at the time. It was the beginning of a fruitful relationship for Elton and him. Buckmaster—who was soon to go on to collaborations with the Rolling Stones, Leonard Cohen, and Miles Davis, and whose career before his death in 2017 took in frequent musical reunions with Elton—always aimed high, and here required a full symphony orchestra.

The first cold gray month of the seventies saw Elton changing the course of his life and career more than anybody involved can have realized. The budget was soon exceeded, and Dudgeon got it increased by playing Dick James half-ready tracks. James heard enough to double down. The album was shaping up as an eclectic but hugely engaging project, from Bernie's rivers of images influenced by poetry, films, and books to Elton's increasingly fluent and charming way of blending his tastes, from gospel to rock to soul, from classical to music hall. Terrific backing vocalists were brought in, like Tony Burrows (known for Edison Lighthouse) and Madeline Bell (Blue Mink). And this time it sounded as big as its dreams: Buckmaster brought multiple extra dimensions, and Dudgeon knew how to switch gears smoothly from song to song. Elton himself pealed with confidence, as if he'd stopped worrying about his career arc and learned to channel any angst or joy directly into the songs and vocals. The production team were both relieved and thrilled when James heard within it what they'd heard, and a buzz scurried around DJM. Dick started treating Elton, who until now he'd effectively indulged, with more courtesy. He remained, of course, sharp enough to tie the singer to a new

In London, 1970: Will this be his year?

ELTON JOHN

TRACK LIST

SIDE ONE
Your Song
I Need You to Turn To
Take Me to the Pilot
No Shoe Strings on Louise
First Episode at Hienton

SIDE TWO
Sixty Years On
Border Song
The Greatest Discovery
The Cage
The King Must Die

Recorded at Trident Studios, London, England
Produced by Gus Dudgeon
Released April 10, 1970
Label DJM Records, DJLPS 406
Highest chart position on release
UK 5, US 4, AUS 4, NLD 2, CAN 4, JPN 40

PERSONNEL
Elton John: piano, vocals, harpsichord (2)
Diana Lewis: Moog synthesizer (5, 9)
Brian Dee: organ (6, 7)
Frank Clark: acoustic guitar (1), double bass (10)
Colin Green: additional guitar (1, 7), Spanish guitar (6)
Clive Hicks: twelve-string guitar (1), rhythm guitar (4), guitar (7, 8, 10), acoustic guitar (9)
Roland Harker: guitar (2)
Alan Parker: rhythm guitar (3)
Caleb Quaye: lead guitar (3, 4, 5), additional guitar (9)
Dave Richmond: bass guitar (1, 7, 8)
Alan Weighall: bass guitar (3, 4, 9)
Les Hurdle: bass guitar (10)
Barry Morgan: drums (1, 3, 4, 7, 9)
Terry Cox: drums (8, 10)
Dennis Lopez: percussion (3, 4)
Tex Navarra: percussion (9)
Skaila Kanga: harp (2, 8)
Paul Buckmaster: cello solo (8), orchestral arrangements and conductor

COVER ART
David Larkham: art direction
Stowell Stanford: photography
Jim Goff: artwork

> "A truly great record . . . superbly crafted songs . . . brilliant production."
>
> RICHARD WILLIAMS, *MELODY MAKER*

Elton dressed in
a leather duster,
playing piano,
1970.

five-year deal, which asked for a level of productivity that seems astonishing compared to modern methods—three albums a year. But the percentages and royalties were, for the era, fair. David Larkham's cover design presented Elton in a kind of sepia blur of shadow, suggesting an artist—bespectacled of course—as intense as Caravaggio. The band and production team appeared overleaf as a motley row of Americana-influenced musicans, Bernie in a ludicrously wide-brimmed hat betraying his Wild West fixation, Elton (with longer hair) joining them in a very of-its-time long, woolly, multicolored scarf. The album's title was simply *Elton John*, as if this was the real debut.

All concerned figured this was an albums act by a serious, chin-stroking singer-songwriter type, and any singles were just an afterthought. First out of the gate, after a democratic discussion, was "Border Song," a decent ballad with spiritual pretensions, released on March 20. It was a sign of the new energy around Elton's name that although it hadn't charted he was invited to perform it on *Top of the Pops*. This he did, hair now cut short, surrounded by dancing girls, with the bonus that he met Dusty Springfield backstage at the Beeb. When she expressed a liking for his song, he declared that had made his year. His year, however, was just lifting off.

Dick James promoted with gusto, setting up a plush launch event at Revolution, then London's hippest club, for March 26. And while in the context of Elton's subsequent stellar sales it felt as if the album only did OK—reaching No. 15—it stuck

around the charts for much of the summer. And this was a chart which saw big hitters like *Let It Be*, *Bridge over Troubled Water*, and *Led Zeppelin II* jockeying for position. *Elton John* passed the ten thousand copies sales mark and put him indisputably on the map rather than the runway. He was known. The reviews were effusive. "A big talent," said *New Musical Express*. At *Melody Maker*, Richard Williams called it "a truly great record," hailing the "superbly crafted songs" and "brilliant production." Williams's ensuing interview included that landmark headline: "Is This the Year of Elton John?"

Well, it might be, if somebody had noticed there was a substantial, if sensitively understated, hit single opening the album. As yet, they flailed: "Rock and Roll Madonna," not from the album, emerged . . . just. The album contained unexploited riches: the lovely ballad "I Need You to Turn To"; the wordy psalm "First Episode at Hienton"; the doomy, grandiose opening to "Sixty Years On" (with Buckmaster's baroque strings and a highly ornate harp); the Stonesy nocturnal shuffle of "The Cage" with its "ah ha woo hooo" refrain. But these weren't perceived as hit-parade candidates. So James urged Elton to bombard the public with live dates to build a following. This wasn't what the singer, going through one of his phases of wobbly confidence regarding performing, had wanted to hear, but he recognized promotion was essential to the cause. He went out as front man of a trio, with—fruitfully—Dee Murray, ex-Mirage, on bass and Nigel Olsson, ex–Plastic Penny, on drums. The two rhythm playerrs were long-haired, contrasting-looking guys who, in truth, looked much more like the seventies' idea of classic rock stars than Elton. The three clicked instantly, both musically and personally. "As soon as we got together, everything felt right," recalled Murray. "It was just like magic." Elton gave them freedom, the bassist said, and never tried to cramp their style. The singer also asked Ray Williams, who had first brought Taupin and himself together, to manage him. After much negotiation with Dick James, an arrangement was agreed whereby Williams did so on behalf of DJM, for a salary and commission.

Touring moved on apace, with the budding new pop sensation sometimes forced to play whatever tatty piano a venue held. However, as hoped, the tough love of the road revived his confidence. In Sweden, he acquired his taste for gigantic hats and jockey caps, fizzing up his image. And supporting Marc Bolan's Tyrannosaurus Rex at London's Roundhouse, his accidental kicking over of his piano stool received a roar of approval. He was canny enough to adopt this as a regular part of his act thereafter. (He was soon to appear with new friend Bolan as T. Rex delivered "Get It On" on *Top of the Pops*, and as T. Rexstacy exploded, appeared in the subsequent *Born to Boogie* movie). According to Keith Hayward's 2013 book *Tin Pan Alley: The Rise of Elton John*, guitar hero Jeff Beck even offered

As soon as we got together, everything felt right. It was just like magic.

DEE MURRAY

LEFT & BELOW: Elton during a portrait session, London, 1970.

to tour with Elton's trio—on condition that, being a big name in America, he took 90 percent of earnings. That, naturally, put Elton off, and had an irked Dick James declaring that his discovery would be out-earning Beck in six months.

Elton kept the faith that James might not be entirely hubristic. He bought increasingly loud clothes from the boutique Mr. Freedom in Kensington Church Street. And then came America, where, in what seemed like the blink of an eye, Elton John really did become a big noise.

A red double-decker bus sporting the large banner "Elton John Has Arrived" took him and the band from the airport to hotel in Los Angeles. This was the idea of Norm Winter, an L.A. publicist whose overzealousness and passion for hype initially rubbed a jetlagged Elton and crew the wrong way. (With hindsight, there's a strong argument that he made Elton's name.) Elton's nerves returned and he threatened to pull out of the scheduled Troubadour shows. The jitters only got worse on

LEFT: Making a statement with ever louder clothes, London, 1970 . . .
BELOW LEFT: . . . and more colorful spectacles, 1970.
BELOW RIGHT: Performing live, London, 1971.
OVERLEAF: Elton, outside a London shop, 1971.

"Rejoice! He's going to be one of rock's biggest and most important stars."

LOS ANGELES TIMES

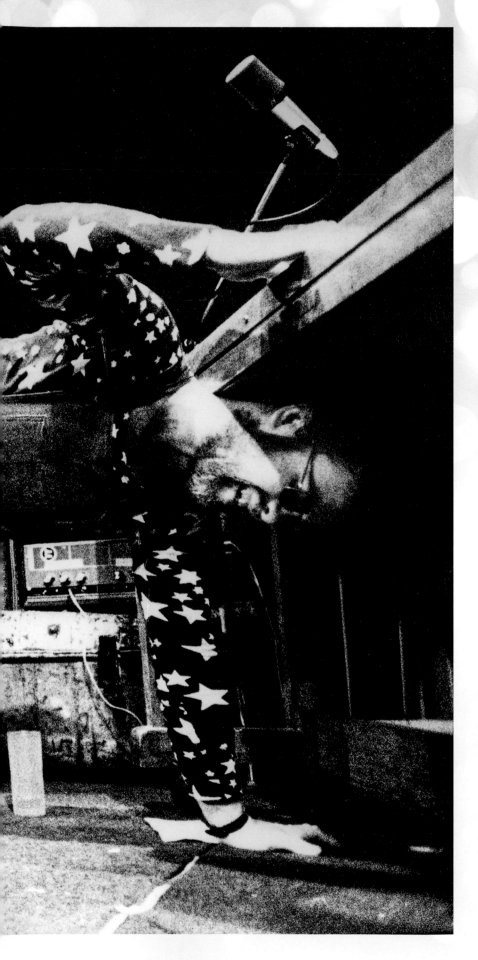

the opening night, when the club filled with names like Quincy Jones, Elmer Bernstein, Henry Mancini, Neil Diamond, David Gates of Bread, Gordon Lightfoot, and Mike Love of the Beach Boys. Winter had done well on the celebrity front. Elton pondered his heroes' proximity and almost crumbled with anxiety. We weren't in Pinner any more, Toto.

Yet of course he got out there and did it, as he had since a very young age. And when the gathering began to mumble distractedly during a run of quieter numbers, he stood up and blasted out some Jerry Lee Lewis-style bluesology. There were cheers and whoops, the audience as surprised as perhaps Elton himself was. It was a triumph. Quincy Jones brought his family backstage to meet him. On the second night, Leon Russell rolled in, a singer-pianist who Elton worshipped, and with whom he developed an enduring musical friendship. Russell invited Elton and Bernie to his house: their first real glimpse of how rock stars lived. They met Brian Wilson too. And then, as the icing on the cake, they read the reviews. Stardom, so long craved, had suddenly rushed in.

And how. Los Angeles had decided Elton John, "a 23-year-old Englishman," was the greatest thing to come out of Britain since Winston Churchill. Phrases like "staggeringly original," "defies classification," and "in every way magnificent" were used. "Rejoice!" declared the *Los Angeles Times*. "He's going to be one of rock's biggest and most important stars." Within a fortnight, the album had sold thirty thousand copies. America loved him. Britain had forged him. But America made him. A full tour was quickly lashed together, and radio stations rotated his tracks. Songwriter Roger Greenaway recalled hearing, while driving in L.A., a radio DJ, before playing one such track, state, "The New Messiah is here."

It was surely about time the New Messiah had a hit single. "Take Me to the Pilot" had become a live favorite, and "No Shoe Strings on Louise" was an amusing Jagger pastiche. In October, the former was released in the States, but radio stations preferred to play its B-side, the previously unassuming "Your Song." Three Dog Night had already released that track on an album, but nobody had fully grasped its potential to connect. It now made the Top 10 in the US, the UK, and plenty of other countries. There was something about it, and Elton, having as a live star gone from slogger to sensation almost overnight, now experienced a similar surge as a recording star. The album too went Top 10 in the US and UK, and as recording had continued prolifically as per Dick James's plans, a third album was conveniently ready to go. *Tumbleweed Connection* was released in October—the same month,

Elton performs at Doug Weston's Troubadour, Los Angeles (now West Hollywood), California, August 25, 1970

TUMBLEWEED CONNECTION

TRACK LIST

SIDE ONE
Ballad of a Well-Known Gun
Come Down in Time
Country Comfort
Son of Your Father
My Father's Gun

SIDE TWO
Where to Now St. Peter?
Love Song
Amoreena
Talking Old Soldiers
Burn Down the Mission

Recorded at Trident Studios, London, England
Produced by Gus Dudgeon
Released October 30, 1970
Label DJM Records, DJLPS 410
Highest chart position on release UK 2, US 5, AUS 4, NLD 4, CAN 4, JPN 30, SPA 7

KEY PERSONNEL
Elton John: lead vocals, piano (1, 3–6, 8, 9, 10), Hammond organ (8), backing vocals (10)
Paul Buckmaster: arrangement, conductor, orchestration
Caleb Quaye: lead guitar (1, 4, 8), acoustic guitar (1, 3, 5), electric guitar (5)
Mike Egan: acoustic guitar (10)
Herbie Flowers: bass guitar (2, 3, 10)
Dave Glover: bass guitar (1, 4, 5, 6)
Chris Laurence: bass guitar (2, 10)
Barry Morgan: drums (2, 3, 10)
Les Thatcher: acoustic guitar (2, 10), twelve-string acoustic guitar (3)

COVER ART
David Larkham: art direction, design, cover design, artwork, photography
Barry Wentzell: photography
Ian Digby-Ovens: photography

> ## Glowing and haunting . . . symptomatic of a new era in pop idols.
>
> *NEW MUSICAL EXPRESS*

confusingly, as "Your Song." So as one album finally unearthed its hit, the next album was arriving at the station.

"Your Song" had filtered through Bernie Taupin's consciousness one early morning as he sat on the roof of 20 Denmark Street, which housed the publishing company where Elton had worked as a hopeful office boy. Its innocent romantic couplets have a wide-eyed charm to which millions have related. And the device whereby the narrator shyly struggles to convey his meaning was, by accident or design, a masterstroke. Paul Buckmaster's string arrangements woo and dissipate any skepticism, while Elton's unshowy chords and Dudgeon's deft use of rhythm laser-guide the message. "Glowing and haunting . . . symptomatic of a new era in pop idols," wrote the *New Musical Express* upon its release, while *Rolling Stone*, not without justification, thought it "McCartney-esque." John Lennon, in a 1975 interview with *Rolling Stone*, famously offered, "I remember hearing 'Your Song' in America—it was one of Elton's first big hits—and thinking: Great, that's the first new thing that's happened since we (the Beatles) happened. It was a step forward. There was something about his vocal that was an improvement on all of the English vocals until then. I was pleased with it." He wasn't alone.

Regarding English vocals, however, Lennon was perhaps overlooking Elton's very American enunciation and phrasings. *Tumbleweed Connection* took the John-Taupin team's fascination with Americana yet further. Cohesively produced by Dudgeon again, with Buckmaster weaving his magic, it nonetheless played with fire by being an unapologetic concept album indulging Taupin's cowboy/gunslinger obsessions. Some thought those were on the way out; others would suggest it was too early in a career to ask the public to listen to your "concept." And that classic sepia Americana shot of a beaten-up Wild West rail

From live star to recording star, 1971.

17-11-70 (US TITLE 11-17-70)

TRACK LIST

SIDE ONE
Take Me to the Pilot
Honky Tonk Women
Sixty Years On
Can I Put You On

SIDE TWO
Bad Side of the Moon
Burn Down the Mission
My Baby Left Me
Get Back

Recorded at A&R Recording Studios, New York, NY, for a live radio broadcast on WABC-FM (later WPLJ)
Produced by Gus Dudgeon
Released April 9, 1971
Label DJM Records, DJLPS 414
Highest chart position on release UK 20, US 11, CAN 10

PERSONNEL
Elton John: piano, lead vocals
Dee Murray: bass, backing vocals
Nigel Olsson: drums, backing vocals

COVER ART
David Larkham

station on the cover? Horsted Keynes, in Sussex, thirty miles south of London.

They'd put the record together at Trident Studios again, most of it recorded in March before all the L.A. madness had kicked off. Indicating how hot the Elton John name was becoming, it reached No. 2 in the UK and 5 in the US, going gold within a year. After "Your Song" had broken the no-hits jinx, it was expected to clinch his superstar status, but yielding no hit singles at all, it landed as more of a holding pattern. Country-tinged, with Taupin referencing multiple cowboys and guns, it's the sound of a songwriting duo wanting to hold on to their rock credibility. John sings with that distinctly Yankee twang—possibly method-acting the lyrics, possibly pandering to his new US fan base—and the influence of the Band's *Music from Big Pink* is discernible throughout. It echoes Little Feat even before Little Feat were truly striding. Album opener "Ballad of a Well-Known Gun" signals his intent, a mid-tempo country-rocker with Caleb Quaye providing tasteful guitar fills and one Dusty Springfield, Elton's heroine, on backing vocals. Themes reoccur across tracks: the gunslingers, a mythical America, reflections on youth and aging in saloons and one-horse towns. "My Father's Gun" and "Talking Old Soldiers" strive to enter the psyche of ailing John Waynes. Yet the best songs are those which transcend, or step aside from, Taupin's fixations. "Come Down in Time" is an exquisite ballad; to this day, despite a sensitive Sting cover, one of John's most underrated tracks. "Where to Now St. Peter?" also has emotional heft, Dudgeon allowing it time to float freely, and the singer liberating a keening falsetto. "Amoreena"—used over the opening sequences of Sidney Lumet's film *Dog Day Afternoon*—bristles with drama, while "Love Song" is a rare case of Elton covering someone else's (good friend Lesley Duncan's) song. The album's climax, "Burn Down the Mission," was soon a live concert showstopper, and here facilitates a grandstand finish, all bombast and infectious enthusiasm. (A version of "Madman Across the Water," put on ice and deselected, though released on reissues, featured Bowie main man Mick Ronson on wailing guitar.) Relatively overlooked within the Elton canon (as far as a million-seller can be overlooked), *Tumbleweed Connection* is a cleverly crafted, impassioned work.

It's not, thankfully, as overlooked, however, as Elton's next two official albums. *Friends* (contracted before fame hit, released late 1970) was a soundtrack album mixing songs and instrumentals, scoring a risqué Lewis Gilbert Anglo-French teen-romance, which got a Golden Globe nomination and even a Grammy nomination for Elton's contribution. The title song made the US Top 40. Hot on its heels came *17-11-70*, an energetic live album recorded from a New York radio broadcast. You can probably guess the date. Initially, this emerged as an East Coast bootleg, the success of which forced the hand of his record labels (DJM in the UK, UNI in the US), who'd planned to later release an edited version. With so many Elton albums now flooding the market, this rushed-out offering suffered commercially, even if it did contain gung-ho readings of the Stones' "Honky Tonk Women" and the Beatles' "Get Back." Even so, Elton has more than once since suggested it's his best live recording, praising the rhythm section (Murray and Olsson). He felt it accurately represented the live rockers his band were, in contrast to the sensitive stylings of "Your Song." In 2017, a full, expanded version of the set was released for Record Store Day, with John's blessing.

It was the next studio album, nonetheless, which while struggling in Britain, struck further chords in America, and included a slow-burning anthem that was only to truly reveal its latent popularity at the turn of the century. "Tiny Dancer" is perhaps the ultimate sleeper hit.

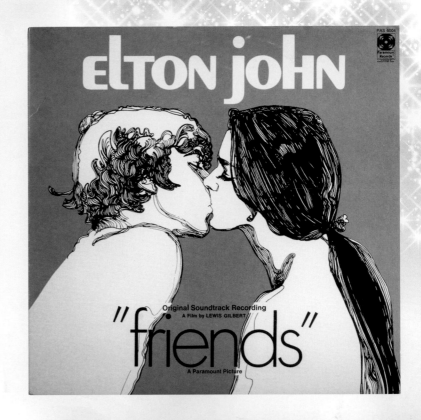

RIGHT: *Friends* soundtrack cover artwork, contracted before fame, 1970.
BELOW: In the studio, 1971.

4

I'M GONNA BE A TEENAGE IDOL

"An engaging entertainment and a nice step forward in phase two of Elton John's career . . . the essence of his personality has always been innocent exuberance."

STEPHEN HOLDEN, *ROLLING STONE*

"I feel more American than British really," Elton said in 1970, and indeed he'd broken the assumed rules of the game by becoming a star in the States before breaking out in his home country. Ray Williams's spell as his manager had ended after disagreements with Dick James, and a cooling-off in his relationship with Elton. The man who had effectively discovered him said, "I could see the kind of manager he needed, and it wasn't someone like me. . . . He was quick, witty and funny, and people just let him do anything he liked. I'd been standing up to him. And that didn't go down very well." Elton, meanwhile, was doing something he'd have liked to do sooner; buying his own flat. "They want me to live in town now," the New Messiah told reporters at the launch of *Tumbleweed Connection*, as if at age twenty-three he was being forcibly press-ganged into moving out of his mum's place.

So he shifted inward from the northwest of London, purchasing a property in a high-end, modern, newly built complex just off Edgware Road. He had a new flatmate too, a twenty-one-year-old Glaswegian, John Reid. Reid had quickly carved out a soaring career at EMI: by age nineteen he'd been the label manager for the UK arm of Tamla Motown and been "romantically" linked to *Carry On* star Barbara Windsor, twelve years his senior. "He wanted it all and you could see he had the chutzpah to go out and get it," she recalled in her memoirs. When Reid first saw Elton play he was bowled over. The two met in San Francisco just as the US critics were eulogizing the singer, and Elton poured out his glee to the nearest Brit. Soon the bonding went further, and they were a couple, both personally and professionally. Dick James saw Reid as a perfect fit for "handling" the new star, while Elton came out to his nearest and dearest regarding his sexuality. His mother and his stepfather, the first people he told, were typically supportive. He's said they always valued honesty, and were understanding and "fabulous." "I was very lucky in that respect. I'm in an industry where it's not unusual for people to be gay, or whatever." He was relieved, while Bernie was just pleased that his working partner was in a committed relationship. Said Dick James, "If he's living with his manager, at least he'll have someone to get him up in the mornings."

Yet Reid's tenacity and temper as he fought Elton's corner with zeal sometimes sat uncomfortably with others. Some described him as ruthless and tough. His own career was to become legendary.

PREVIOUS PAGE: Elton John performing a handstand on his piano, London, 1972.
ABOVE: Elton leans on Bernie, on the beach, California, 1972.

Bernie too had grown into changes. He'd fallen in love with Maxine Feibelman, and the pair married in Market Rasen in March 1971. Maxine was soon to be immortalized in the lyric to "Tiny Dancer," as the "seamstress." The wedding reception was boosted by unlimited champagne supplied by Maxine's father, a champagne importer. The newlyweds bought a cottage in Tealby.

1971 was the first year John and Taupin had begun as celebrated stars, yet their work ethic only escalated. Elton toured relentlessly, especially in America, and somehow found a spare moment or two to produce one side of old pal John Baldry's latest album *It Ain't Easy*, with Rod Stewart producing the other. Bernie too got into extracurricular production, helming David Ackles's *American Gothic*, still thought of by some as a neglected classic. He made his own first album as well, persuaded by DJM, though it made little headway, and even Taupin soon seemed to want it forgotten.

It did feature guitarist Davey Johnstone, who now expanded Elton's trio to a quartet, and was in time to become his longest-serving musician. The Scot's talent had been spotted by Gus Dudgeon, who brought him in to Trident Studios during early '71 to play on Elton's next album. Dudgeon at this stage maintained that the live setup wasn't ideal for recording, and preferred to assemble his own choice of top musos. Among them were names like pianist Rick Wakeman, bassist Herbie Flowers, and guitarist Chris Spedding, as well as percussionist Ray Cooper. Cooper would have further parts to play in the Elton story. Elton himself stuck solely to piano (and vocals) here. Engineering was one Ken Scott, who was at around the same time quietly settling in as David Bowie's producer on *Hunky Dory* and *Ziggy Stardust*. Scott wasn't alone in eulogizing Paul Buckmaster's orchestral arrangements.

Madman Across the Water was released on November 5 and—again lacking an obvious hit single and jumping between blues, country, and symphonic rock—made a greater impression in the US than in the UK. In fact, it stalled outside the Top 40 in Britain, but made No. 8 in America, swiftly going gold, and hung around long enough to be the tenth-best seller of 1972. "Levon" was the first single; "Tiny Dancer" the second. The title track, a new version of a song previously recorded during the *Tumbleweed Connection* sessions, on which Mick Ronson had guested, was now less feral, with Buckmaster's strings to the fore. (Rumors abounded that the titular character was President Richard Nixon, but Taupin never confirmed them.) Dudgeon did suggest that "Levon" was inspired by the Band's singer-drummer Levon Helm, a hero of the writing duo, but again Taupin declined to back this up. Jon Bon Jovi later covered it and declared it his favorite song of all time. "Indian Sunset" received a second life when it was sampled by Eminem for Tupac Shakur's posthumous rap hit "Ghetto Gospel" in 2005. Elton, for his part, has let on that at this stage he still had to do quite a bit of editing with Taupin's sometimes abstract words, and that his colleague was still learning in terms of song-craft, verse-chorus structures, and the like. There can be little doubt nowadays that both nailed it on what's become the album's generation-crossing golden great. "Tiny Dancer," with B. J. Cole on pedal-steel, survives as one of Elton's best-loved songs.

Taupin tried to capture the feel and impressions of life, largely on the road, in California. With a healthy interest in women, "Tiny Dancer" fuses the wide-eyed innocence of the farm boy with the joie de vivre of a young man starting to see all his wildest fantasies come true. Overlong as a single, it didn't make much impact upon birth. Yet almost three decades later, in 2000, its prominent appearance in the Cameron Crowe film *Almost Famous*, an idealized love letter to the early-seventies US rock scene, projected onto the song an entirely fresh set of dance moves. As the twenty-first century dawned, it seemed as if everybody, not just Kate Hudson and Billy Crudup, was claiming to have known every word all along.

Madman Across the Water, which Kate Bush has declared a personal favorite ("I had a bit of a crush on Elton John . . . before he got really famous") emphasized Elton and Bernie's transatlantic themes (musically and lyrically) and the American audience lapped it up. There remained an element of frustration,

Sporting a musical sweater, 1972.

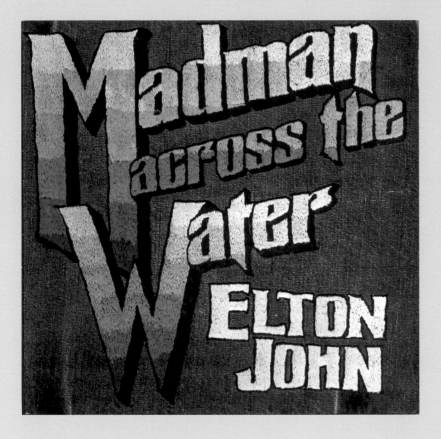

MADMAN ACROSS THE WATER

TRACK LIST

SIDE ONE
Tiny Dancer
Levon
Razor Face
Madman Across the Water

SIDE TWO
Indian Sunset
Holiday Inn
Rotten Peaches
All the Nasties
Goodbye

Recorded at Trident Studios, London, England
Produced by Gus Dudgeon
Released November 5, 1971
Label DJM Records, DJLPH 420
Highest chart position on release
UK 41, US 8, CAN 9, AUS 8, ITA 14, JPN 13, SPA 11

PERSONNEL

Elton John: piano, vocals
Brian Dee: harmonium (2)
Rick Wakeman: Hammond organ (3, 4, 7)
Jack Emblow: accordion (3)
Diana Lewis: ARP synthesizer (4, 7)
Caleb Quaye: electric guitar (1, 2, 3), acoustic guitar (6)
B. J. Cole: steel guitar (1)
Davey Johnstone: acoustic guitar (1, 4, 7), mandolin (6), sitar (6)
Chris Spedding: electric guitar (4), slide guitar (7)
David Glover: bass guitar (1, 3, 6)
Brian Odgers: bass guitar (2)
Herbie Flowers: bass guitar (4, 5, 7)
Chris Laurence: double bass (5)
Dee Murray: bass guitar (8)
Roger Pope: drums (1, 3, 6)
Barry Morgan: drums (2)
Terry Cox: drums (4, 5, 7)
Nigel Olsson: drums (8)
Ray Cooper: percussion (4), tambourine (7, 8)
Paul Buckmaster: orchestral arrangements and conductor (1, 2, 4, 5, 6, 8, 9)
David Katz: orchestra contractor
Lesley Duncan, Sue & Sunny, Barry St. John, Liza Strike, Roger Cook, Tony Burrows, Terry Steele, Dee Murray, Nigel Olsson: backing vocals (1, 6, 7)
Cantores em Ecclesia Choir: backing vocals (5, 8)
Robert Kirby: choir director

> "'Tiny Dancer' has the delicate melody, virtuoso singing, and innovative arranging that have marked Elton John since 'Your Song.'"
>
> *ROLLING STONE*

COVER ART
David Larkham: art direction, design, illustrations, photography, cover photo
Bob Gruen: photography

though, in the failure to find a more noticeable niche in Britain. Luckily, the next single was to fly high as a kite.

Much as he'd have liked them, hit singles and UK success evidently weren't crucial. With John Reid he'd splashed some cash (which was to become a habit) and moved in early 1972 to a salubrious new home in "the stockbroker belt," a short journey from London in Surrey's Virginia Water. They had vast gardens and a swimming pool. A games room. A Rolls Royce. Gold discs in the toilet. Hanging out with movie star friends. It was a proper rock star abode. And less than two years before, he and Bernie were crashing in Elton's mum's maisonette. He'd now bought Sheila a house in Ickenham and a fancy car.

His own house's name, Elton had decided, should be Hercules. He liked the name so much that in January '72 he formally changed his own by deed poll. Elton Hercules John couldn't bear people calling him Reg: even when rock star peers did it by accident, having always known him as that, he chafed. In a pop world exploding from black and white to the rich colors of glam, big statement names were all the rage. Ziggy and Alvin Stardust. Alice Cooper. Gary Glitter. Barry Blue. Nothing was too loud or camp or silly. And if the planet had decided that Reg was a superstar, then he had to commit to a befitting name. The irony was that while other *Top of the Pops* regulars pretended to be gay, Elton was pretending (outside the circle of friends and family) to be straight. He was also bemoaning the "singer-songwriter" label, arguing that pop music should be "entertainment" and not "an art form." He stressed that he wanted his music from now on to represent a band, not something that people took too seriously. Thus, the next album was pitched by Bernie as "funky," with fewer opulent strings. It would, he added, "shock a few people." They claimed they were going back to their roots. Realistically, this would have meant a pub in Pinner, but now the team decided against Trident and recorded at the Château d'Hérouville in the French countryside, twenty miles north of Paris. David Bowie, Iggy Pop, and T. Rex were among those to also layer the legend of this location through music's boldest decade.

At twenty-one, Scottish guitarist Davey Johnstone was now a band member, and, it seemed, a good luck charm. All involved wanted to make a record that felt more like one made by a touring band and less like a showcase for session men. They wanted it to sound lighter and breezier than its predecessors, and embrace pop. Removed from their previous studio comfort zone, the entourage lived at the Château (nicknamed Strawberry Studios) for the duration. The team gelled well. Elton would knock up

LEFT: In his new home (vast garden and swimming pool not shown), 1972.
RIGHT: Performing on BBC's *Sounds for Saturday*, December, 1971.

> " I had a bit of a crush on Elton John . . . before he got really famous.

KATE BUSH

melodies to Bernie's lyrics in the morning and the band would then record them that day. Ken Scott, not one to need to gild the lily of an anecdote, has recalled that he witnessed Elton writing "Rocket Man" in a matter of minutes over breakfast, with Elton chopping and changing Bernie's lyrics as he saw fit. Bernie fully accepted this. The net result was an album, *Honky Château*, that succeeded both as a leap into a new area—revealing a more accessible, pop-conscious side to Elton John—and as a commercial gambit. It went to No. 1 in the US and No. 2 in the UK. They didn't lose their early fans. They just acquired more.

HONKY CHÂTEAU

TRACK LIST

SIDE ONE
Honky Cat
Mellow
I Think I'm Going to Kill Myself
Susie (Dramas)
Rocket Man (I Think It's Going to Be a Long, Long Time)

SIDE TWO
Salvation
Slave
Amy
Mona Lisas and Mad Hatters
Hercules

Recorded at Château d'Hérouville, Hérouville, France; mixed at Trident Studios, London, England
Produced by Gus Dudgeon
Released May 19, 1972
Label DJM Records, DJLPH 423
Highest chart position on release
UK 2, US 1, CAN 3, AUS 4, NLD 9, ITA 5, JPN 21, SPA 1, GER 43, NOR 8

PERSONNEL
Elton John: vocals, piano (2–6 and 8–10), Fender Rhodes (1), Hammond organ (2, 4), harmonium (6)
Davey Johnstone: guitar (2–10), banjo (1, 7), steel guitar (7) mandolin (9), backing vocals (3, 5, 6, 8, 10)
Dee Murray: bass guitar, backing vocals (3, 5, 6, 8, 10)
Nigel Olsson: drums (1–8 and 10), congas (7), tambourine, backing vocals (3, 5, 6, 8, 10)
Ivan Jullien: trumpet (1)
Jacques Bolognesi: trombone (1)
Jean-Louis Chautemps, Alain Hatot: saxophone (1)
Jean-Luc Ponty: electric violin (2, 8)
"Legs" Larry Smith: tap dance (3)
David Hentschel: ARP synthesizer (5, 10)
Ray Cooper: congas (8)
Gus Dudgeon: whistle, backing vocals (10)
Madeline Bell, Liza Strike, Larry Steel, Tony Hazzard: backing vocals (6)

COVER ART
Ed Caraeff

"A really important album for us. We'd made it, but we still had one final bridge to cross, which was to make a great album."

ELTON JOHN

The subject of ITV's documentary series, *Aquarius*, 1972.

Elton described it as a very important album to have made, seeing it as a crucial step in the desired journey from success to artistic greatness. He wanted to cross that bridge. While some might have missed the mesmeric contributions of Paul Buckmaster to the earlier work, it yielded hits and a new home away from home. The Château—they liked it so much they adapted its name for the title—was to host the ensemble again for the next two albums.

Honky Château stands up as one of Elton's most eclectic, durable collections. Its legend is assured by the inclusion of "Rocket Man," but it witnesses the star finding the perfect-for-him balance between camp pop rock and gushing ballads that would serve his ensuing career so well—that tricky tightrope walk between sincerity and glibness. "Rocket Man" somehow appeased both categories. A curious modern classic,

clearly indebted to Bowie's "Space Oddity" (which Dudgeon had produced), its melodic strength and air of sadness are undeniable. Bernie's lyrics had come to him during a car trip to his mum's. Yet as with "Your Song," the human frailty spoke to listeners. "Honky Cat" was a flippant piano boogie in the style of Dr. John, while deeper, darker shades came through as Bernie got serious. "I Think I'm Going to Kill Myself" was a satire on teen angst, but touched a few sensitive nerves along its way. "Susie (Dramas)" was another song about infatuation; it grappled with grit beneath its honky-tonk playfulness. "Salvation" was a slight return to the white gospel they'd dabbled in before, picking at religion, and "Slave" saw Taupin revisiting his Americana obsessions. On "Amy," Jagger's influence could be heard again in Elton's vocals.

Otherwise, it was on the outstanding "Mona Lisas and Mad Hatters" that the writing pair's talent clicked most effectively. It could have come across as maudlin and psalm-like, yet instead it resonates. The mood's broken, however, by the doo-wop

LEFT: Princess Margaret and Lord Snowdon meet Elton John backstage at a benefit concert, the Shaw Theatre, London, February 27, 1972.
BELOW: Performing onstage with his hat on the piano, 1972.
RIGHT: Elton John plays piano as he performs onstage, 1972.

LEFT: Elton and Marc Bolan of T. Rex performing on the BBC's *Top of the Pops,* London, December 1971.
RIGHT: Elton, Marc Bolan and Ringo Starr promote the film *Born to Boogie* in 1972.

finale of "Hercules" (that name again). In terms of Elton's rise to the top ranks, *Honky Château* put the cherry on the cake. And "Rocket Man" has stayed in orbit for such a long, long time that, decades on, the 2019 Elton John biopic takes its name. Varying tales suggest Bernie's lyric was inspired by Ray Bradbury's short story "The Rocket Man" or by Taupin observing a shooting star. Kate Bush covered the song in 1991, describing such as "fulfilling a dream."

Another superstar, Marc Bolan, had in March '72 invited Elton to appear in his movie *Born to Boogie*. With T. Rextasy and Bolanmania at their peak, this was a more than useful hook-up, lending Elton charisma and credibility by association. He described Marc as both a dear friend and a larger-than-life rock star from another planet. Elton had guested with T. Rex on a Christmas 1971 edition of *Top of the Pops*, playing piano on "Get It On" (Rick Wakeman had played it on the single, though Wakeman has admitted he did very little and that Marc and producer Tony Visconti were just kindly helping him pay

his rent that week with his fee). In the patchy but entertaining Ringo Starr–directed film, Elton joined in on "Children of the Revolution" and Little Richard's "Tutti Frutti." He and Marc were to engage in a friendly rivalry over the next year or three, bantering over who was the bigger star. They'd even send each other life-size cardboard cutout promos of themselves, often as birthday presents, but with an undercurrent of true competitiveness. At first, Bolan was the bigger sensation, but he never truly broke into the American market, while Elton was to explode over there. The way things panned out might have been a bitter pill for Marc to swallow.

Elton's never-resting recording schedule continued at a pace that seems deranged viewed from the perspective of today's rules of releasing and marketing. The four-piece band, enjoying their personal and musical chemistry, were back at the Château in June '72 for the sixth studio album, which landed in record shops in January '73. *Don't Shoot Me I'm Only the Piano Player* became Britain's biggest-selling album of that year, beating the

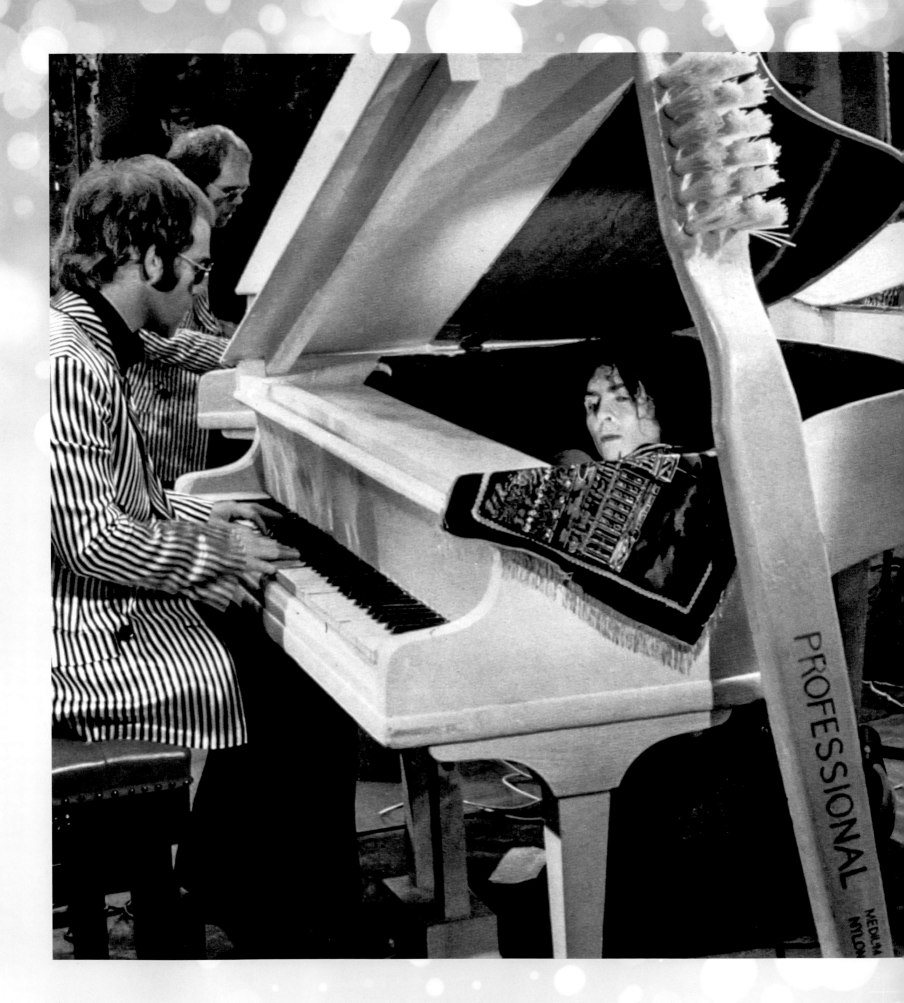

On the set of *Born to Boogie*, 1972.

Elton's vocal is unusually tender and expressive.

STEPHEN HOLDEN, *ROLLING STONE*

likes of *Aladdin Sane* and *The Dark Side of the Moon* to that honor. Its numbers couldn't be argued with: an American No. 1 (now triple platinum), Elton's first UK No. 1, plus "Crocodile Rock" snapping up his first US chart-topper. "Daniel" reached No. 2 there. In Britain, both glided into the top five. The piano player was taking his shot. That knowing title popped up during a night out that the now A-list celebrity Elton spent with none other than Groucho Marx. After hours of Groucho taking the mickey as only he could, quipping that John Elton had his name the wrong way round, Elton blurted the line out. It was possibly a bewildered comic mishmash of the name of Truffaut's 1960 film *Shoot the Piano Player* and the (perhaps apocryphal) Oscar Wilde quote, "Don't shoot the piano player—he's doing his best."

Elton's years of pub work now helped sustain his prolific schedule. "Crocodile Rock" was an homage to the fifties' rock and roll records he had grown up adoring, and his voice aimed to emulate Bobby Vee, falsetto flung high. It also owed a debt to Australian band Daddy Cool's sizeable hit "Eagle Rock" and Pat Boone's hit "Speedy Gonzales," by composer Buddy Kaye. "Of course it's a rip-off," explained Elton himself in the liner notes to a 1995 reissue of the album. "It's derivative in every sense of the word." "High Flying Bird" bore aspirations to resemble Van Morrison (and lent its name to a later Noel Gallagher band), while "Midnight Creeper" was Rolling Stones-esque. Yet John comes across as cheerful, darting between voices and styles. He was now comfortable and happy with the band and with his "arrived" status. Dudgeon brought in a horn section for the lively, catchy "Elderberry Wine," while Paul Buckmaster returned to adorn "Blues for My Baby and Me" and "Have Mercy on the Criminal" with his characteristically charismatic strings. "I'm Gonna Be a Teenage Idol" nodded and winked to Elton's friend Marc Bolan, the brightest, born-to-boogie superstar of the year. Of the album as a whole (tastefully packaged in a sleeve that

Autographing albums for fans, London, 1973.

referenced Hollywood's allure and mystery), *Rolling Stone*'s Stephen Holden opined, "an engaging entertainment and a nice step forward in phase two of Elton John's career. . . . The essence of his personality has always been innocent exuberance." The review also remarked upon Bernie's "often impenetrable" lyrics and feared that on occasion they, along with Dudgeon's "overly lavish production" were denying the artist a larger audience. Well, this was no longer an issue. The audience could hardly get much larger. Damning with faint praise, though not without justification, the magazine summed Elton up as the current "bantamweight" champion of rock and roll.

If there's a claim to more gravitas and grandeur than that, perhaps "Daniel" was its greatest melodic murmur. Kept from No. 1 in the States (where MCA Records had swallowed

UNI and was thus Elton's label there) by Paul McCartney and Wings' "My Love," it won the 1973 Ivor Novello award for its authors. Taupin's original source was a newspaper article about a wounded Vietnam vet. He reckoned, years later, that it was his most "misinterpreted" song of all. It had nothing to do with any actual brother of his, though he's suggested the narrator could be Daniel's brother. Neither was it conceived as a gay anthem, or a paean to the joys of Spain. "The story was about a guy who went back to a small town in Texas, returning from the Vietnam War. They'd lauded him, treated him like he was a hero. But he just wanted to go home, go back to the farm, and try to get back to the life that he'd led before. I wanted to write something sympathetic to the people that came home." As that thoughtful *Rolling Stone* review put it, it also utilized some pioneering keyboard sounds, and was "the album's most moving cut. A gem of technical virtuosity, it has Elton doubling on electric piano and 'flute' mellotron and Ken Scott on synthesizer, together

DON'T SHOOT ME I'M ONLY THE PIANO PLAYER

TRACK LIST

SIDE ONE
Daniel
Teacher I Need You
Elderberry Wine
Blues for My Baby and Me
Midnight Creeper

SIDE TWO
Have Mercy on the Criminal
I'm Gonna Be a Teenage Idol
Texan Love Song
Crocodile Rock
High Flying Bird

Recorded at Château d'Hérouville, Hérouville, France; mixed at Trident Studios, London, England
Produced by Gus Dudgeon
Released January 26, 1973
Label DJM Records, DJLPH 427
Highest chart position on release UK 1, US 1, CAN 1, AUS 1, NLD 2, ITA 1, JPN 4, SPA 1, GER 16, NOR 1

PERSONNEL
Elton John: vocals, piano (2–4, 6, 7, 9, 10), Fender Rhodes (1, 5), Leslie piano (7), Farfisa, Hammond organ (track 9), harmonium (8), mellotron (1, 2)
Davey Johnstone: acoustic guitar, electric guitar, Leslie guitar; banjo (1), sitar (4), mandolin (8), backing vocals (2, 7, 10)
Dee Murray: bass guitar, backing vocals (2, 7, 10)
Nigel Olsson: drums, maracas (1), backing vocals (2, 7, 10)
Ken Scott: ARP synthesizer (1)
Gus Dudgeon: brass arrangement (3, 5, 7)
Paul Buckmaster: orchestral arrangement (4, 6)
Jacques Bolognesi: trombone (3, 5, 7)
Ivan Jullien: trumpet (3, 5, 7)
Jean-Louis Chautemps, Alain Hatot: saxophone (3, 5, 7)

COVER ART
David Larkham and Michael Ross: art direction and sleeve design
Ed Caraeff: cover photo

> "A gem of technical virtuosity . . . making as deft use of the new electronic instrumentation as I've heard."

STEPHEN HOLDEN, *ROLLING STONE*, ON "DANIEL"

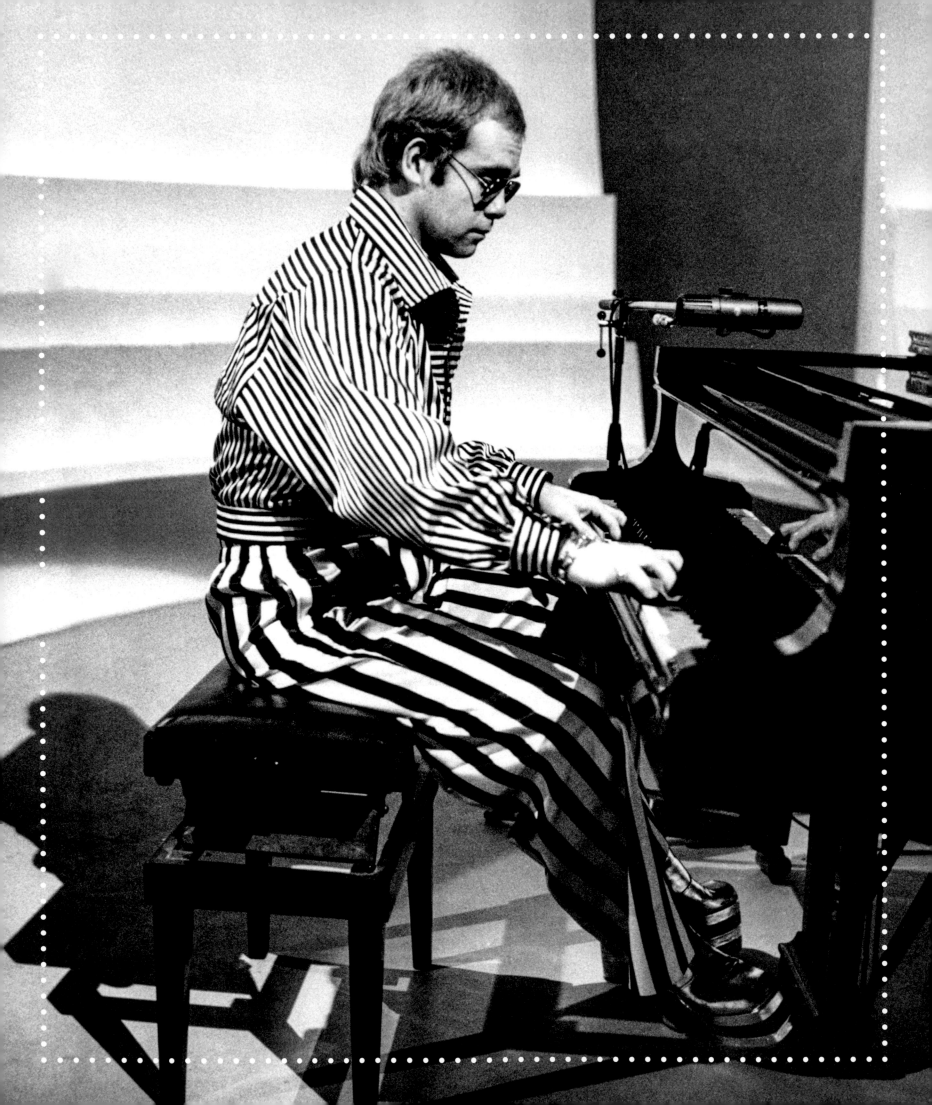

making as deft use of the new electronic instrumentation as I've heard. Elton's vocal is unusually tender and expressive."

The road went on. The next (double) album—these guys weren't short of ideas and energy, their output veering towards the manic—has come to be generally (if, in my opinion, erroneously) cited as Elton's best, and with over thirty million copies sold, is his biggest seller of all. *Goodbye Yellow Brick Road* wasn't planned as a double; the Château simply bombarded the boys with the muse. By accident or design, what to most people is the definitive Elton John work ensued.

Bernie had written all the lyrics in just over two weeks, while Elton knocked up all the music in three days while residing at the Pink Flamingo Hotel in Kingston, Jamaica. The original idea had been to record the album in Jamaica, following the example set by the Rolling Stones with *Goat's Head Soup*. They started preliminary work there, but local unrest made matters difficult. There were technical issues with the studio and Elton didn't warm to the in-house piano. On top of this, the recent heavyweight boxing bout between Joe Frazier and George Foreman was causing disturbances in Kingston, and there were ongoing political tensions in the area, fueled by the economic situation. Bernie later recalled (in the *To Be Continued* box set booklet), "If I remember rightly, the studio was surrounded by barbed wire and guys with machine guns."

And so the team adjourned back to the Château d'Hérouville, where they put down this plethora of songs in a fortnight, with seventeen (if the opulent, segued opener counts as one) from twenty-two making the final cut. The working title shifted between "Vodka and Tonics" and "Silent Movies, Talking Pictures" before it was all yellow. Gus Dudgeon said it was never planned as a double, but John and Taupin were at their prolific peak. Bernie played with imagery concerning cinema and old Hollywood, reaching to capture a sense of nostalgia for childhood, his young idealism, and things lost.

LEFT: In Rome, 1973
BELOW: Onstage, Hammersmith Odeon, London, 1973.

GOODBYE YELLOW BRICK ROAD

TRACK LIST

SIDE ONE
Funeral for a Friend/Love Lies Bleeding
Candle in the Wind
Bennie and the Jets

SIDE TWO
Goodbye Yellow Brick Road
This Song Has No Title
Grey Seal
Jamaica Jerk-Off
I've Seen That Movie Too

SIDE THREE
Sweet Painted Lady
The Ballad of Danny Bailey (1909-34)
Dirty Little Girl
All the Girls Love Alice

SIDE FOUR
Your Sister Can't Twist (But She Can Rock 'n' Roll)
Saturday Night's Alright for Fighting
Roy Rogers
Social Disease
Harmony

Recorded at Château d'Hérouville, Hérouville, France;
remixed and overdubbed at Trident Studios, London, England
Produced by Gus Dudgeon
Released October 5, 1973
Label DJM Records, DJLPD 1001
Highest chart position on release UK 1, US 1, CAN 1,
AUS 1, ITA 5, JPN 22, SPA 8, GER 41, NOR 5

PERSONNEL
Elton John: vocals, piano (1–6, 8–10, 12–17), Fender Rhodes (5, 6),
Hammond organ (3, 7), Farfisa (5, 13), mellotron (5, 6, 11), Leslie
piano (11), tack piano (uncredited) on "Social Disease"
Dee Murray: bass guitar
Davey Johnstone: acoustic guitar, electric guitar, Leslie, slide guitar,
steel guitar, banjo
Nigel Olsson: drums, congas, tambourine
Dee Murray, Davey Johnstone, Nigel Olsson: backing vocals (1, 2,
4, 10, 13, 17)
Del Newman: orchestral arrangement (4, 8–10, 15, 17)
Leroy Gómez: saxophone solo (16)
David Hentschel: ARP synthesizer (1, 12)
Kiki Dee: backing vocals on "All the Girls Love Alice"
Ray Cooper: tambourine on "All the Girls Love Alice"

> "The first time I'd ever recorded standing up, singing and leaping around in the studio, going crazy."
>
> ELTON JOHN

COVER ART
David Larkham and Michael Ross: art direction and
sleeve design

Not one to lack hubris, Elton grandly described *Goodbye Yellow Brick Road* as his *White Album*. And it did shunt him into a Beatles-like levels of popularity, especially Stateside. In reality it's a mixed magnum opus, that would have likely been tighter as a single album. It did show us a star at his creative busiest. Yet with the distance of hindsight, today, the famous sections sound great while the numerous fillers (of which there are more than is usually acknowledged) sound flimsy, betraying the rush job. Flush with confidence whatever the geography, Jamaica or France, Elton managed to concoct a largely invigorating brew of rock, pop, glam (the genre of the moment, or of recent moments, though it was arguably already on the way out), music hall, and reggae.

The epic Wagnerian strains of the "Funeral for a Friend" instrumental lead into the red-meat refrains of "Love Lies Bleeding," where Johnstone's guitars, now a key element of the band's sound, give wings to a song that echoes the glam swagger effortlessly embodied by peers like Bolan and Bowie. An irresistible run of now world-renowned standards follows, with "Candle in the Wind" (then a homage to Marilyn Monroe, later of course retooled as tribute to Princess Diana); the glitter-soul stomp of "Bennie and the Jets" (possibly a fuzzy stab at a Ziggy and the Spiders fantasy); and the plaintive title song, in which Bernie, who should have listened to his old man, autobiographically eulogizes the virtues of country mice over city rats.

After the melodically rich "This Song Has No Title", the results are more uneven. This is a very top-loaded double album. "Jamaica Jerk-Off" and "Dirty Little Girl" will not star on any "Best of" compilations. "Grey Seal" was a functional remake of an earlier B-side. Side three (as was) perked up with the workable "The Ballad of Danny Bailey." There's a slight upswing in the final quarter. "Saturday Night's Alright for Fighting" transcends its Who-influenced glam-buzz, and "Harmony" is a deft closer. It was mooted as a single but its predecessors (like the album) stuck around on the charts so long that the next job lot were on the way before it got its chance.

Released on October 5, 1973, with Ian Beck's now iconic artwork showing platform-booted, satin-jacketed Elton stepping into a poster of a scene depicting that Oz-like yellow brick road, the album was certified gold within a month. It was America's biggest seller of the year, and its four major hit singles are landmarks of the era. "Saturday Night's Alright for Fighting" rocked up first, its picture sleeve giving us Elton swigging booze from a bottle. While it's a stretch to think of him as a lad getting into scraps, Bernie had put together the riff-happy song's tale from memories of testy teenage nights in Market Rasen's Aston Arms. Johnstone's abrasive guitar makes it sound convincing. "The first time I'd ever recorded standing up, singing and leaping around the studio, going crazy," recalled Elton.

Still from *Elton John and Bernie Taupin Say Goodbye to Norma Jean and Other Things* TV show, 1973.

By contrast, the album's title track wafted out next, its soft rock charm sweetly seductive. Tapping into *The Wizard of Oz*—the first film Bernie ever saw—and the trials of Dorothy and gang, it attests that going back to a simpler, quieter life is the way forward. Fun as the road can often be, there's no place like home. After a detour into the jaunty jingle bells of the seasonal release "Step into Christmas," which has enjoyed a lengthy afterlife even if it didn't exactly tear down chimneys in its first year, the next single was "Candle in the Wind," which reasserted Elton's earnestness (at least in the UK; in the States "Bennie and the Jets" was chosen). Taupin said in a later Eagle Vision documentary on the album that the song remembered the late "Norma Jean" (he admitted to being a Marilyn fanatic), as well as pondering "the idea of fame or youth or somebody being cut short in the prime of their life. It could have been about James Dean, or Montgomery Clift. It could have been about Jim Morrison. How we glamorize death, how we immortalize people." In 1997, it was to be re-addressed, and to become a populist anthem.

Elton didn't want "Bennie and the Jets" to be a single, but in America it gave him another No. 1, even infiltrating the *Billboard* Soul chart, and to his delight it granted him an appearance on *Soul Train* in '75. Dudgeon's use of a layered, reverbed "live applause" track (which borrowed some sounds from Jimi Hendrix's live album *Isle of Wight*) was little short of visionary.

And as applause bombarded Elton from every angle, his career was everything he'd dreamed of during the youthful years of struggle. He was one of the biggest stars in the world. When was he going to land?

BELOW: Elton John holds the plaque commemorating his induction into the Madison Square Garden Hall of Fame in New York, October, 1973. John, who broke the Garden's all-time concert attendance record and recorded a gold album at the arena, joined the ranks of P. T. Barnum, Gene Autry, and Willis Reed in the Hall of Fame.
RIGHT: In a flamboyant stage outfit of white suit with feather trim and rhinestone encrusted glasses, 1973.

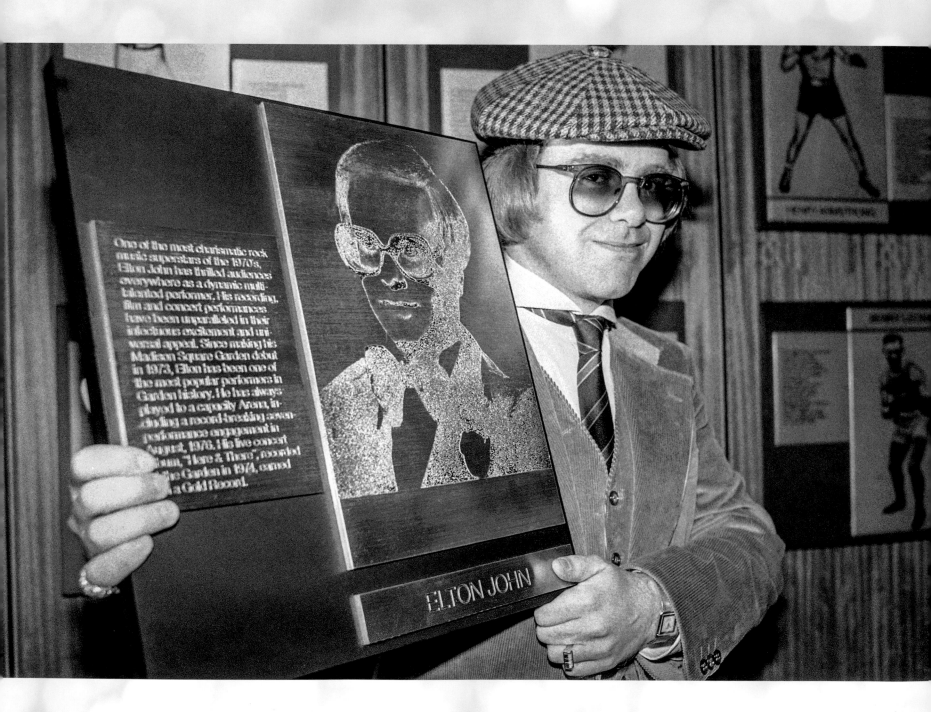

5

TELL ME
WHEN THE
WHISTLE
BLOWS

"Probably my finest album, because it wasn't commercial in any way. We did have songs such as 'Someone Saved My Life Tonight,' which is one of the best songs that Bernie and I have ever written together, but whether a [six-minute] song like that could be a single these days is questionable. [The album] was written from start to finish in running order, as a kind of story about coming to terms with failure—or trying desperately not to be one. We lived that story."

ELTON JOHN

Trouble, as is its wont, was hiding around the next bend. While the going was good though, Elton launched his very own record label, Rocket. Drinking red wine one late night at the Château d'Hérouville with Davey Johnstone, he decided this was a marvelous idea. Announced in September 1972, Rocket was owned by John Reid, Bernie Taupin, Gus Dudgeon, and Steve Brown, and was dedicated to nurturing new talent. Or as Elton told *Disc*, "What we're offering is individual love and devotion, a fucking good royalty for the artist and a company that works its bollocks off." The company had its offices on Wardour Street, and was managed by Brown, while Reid now helmed his own firm, John Reid Enterprises, in Mayfair. Among the artists backed by Rocket were folk-proggers Stackridge (who later spawned the Korgis), Eurythmic-of-the-future Dave Stewart, Colin Blunstone, not-exactly-new-talent Neil Sedaka, and the label's first hit-maker, Kiki Dee. Born Pauline Matthews, Kiki had been, at a young age, the first Brit signed to Motown. The quality of her voice was indisputable. When she first went to meet Elton at his home, Neil Young was visiting, and Kiki made an impression by (accidentally) dropping and smashing a set of wine glasses on the floor. This was sufficient to encourage Elton to produce her *Loving and Free* album. The moving and intimate "Amoureuse" (co-written by Gary Osborne, who in subsequent years would become Elton's writing partner) broke into the charts after a slow start to give Kiki her first chart success and got the champagne bottles popping at Rocket.

The label's official launch party, in April 1973, forsook London glamour and swept guests away on a train to a small town in the Cotswolds. Elton's eccentricities were now an essential part of his appeal, and his onstage costumes grew increasingly berserk. His hair would be bright orange one day, turquoise the next. His fortune was made, and he was rich enough to buy expensive works of art by Rembrandt and Francis Bacon. He was in the zone, in the sweet spot where his creativity meshed perfectly with the commercial arena. "I could fart and reach number one," he's said, rather demystifying the process. While *Goodbye Yellow Brick Road* was in residence at No. 1 around the globe, he was still exuberant enough to pull off madcap stunts. Iggy Pop, of all people, has recalled that one night onstage during a Stooges tour he glanced to his left, hungover, to see a large guy in a gorilla suit lumbering towards him. It was Elton, who removed the gorilla head, picked Iggy up in a hug and danced happily about. Iggy has reflected that he was irritated at the time and Elton was lucky that nobody in the band, particularly its front man, knocked him out before knowing who he was.

The conveyor belt of carnival days couldn't last forever. Success bred excess, as so often in the seventies, and Elton's first burst of the fantasy life began to hit the buffers as he felt the relentless pressure. The numbers hadn't given any indication of this: on the surface everything was thriving. He signed a massive ($8 million) deal with MCA in 1974, and in November they put out a *Greatest Hits* album. Despite the familiarity of the tracks, it was America's top-selling album of 1975 and Elton's first to pass the 10 million sales mark there. It's now sold over 24 million. And earlier that year the follow-up to *Goodbye Yellow Brick Road* had, almost as a matter of course, raced to No. 1 in both the US and the UK, yielding two of Elton's most anthemic hits and winning a Grammy nomination. Yet, arguably, this was the first small worm in the too-good-to-be-true apple.

PREVIOUS PAGE: Elton performs at an open-air concert in Watford, England, May 1974.
ABOVE: At home in Wentworth, England, during a shoot for the cover of *Greatest Hits,* 1974.

Caribou, released June 1974, was named after Caribou Ranch in Colorado where some of the recording took place that January, though other sessions took place in Santa Monica and back at Trident in London. Both Elton and producer Gus Dudgeon have come clean that it was rushed to a ridiculous degree, given touring commitments and the like. The singer's recalled there was "enormous pressure," with a Japanese tour looming. And on the peculiar track "Solar Prestige a Gammon," Bernie, encouraged by Elton, had deliberately written a litany of nonsense just to take the mickey out of over-earnest fans and song analysts. Dudgeon went further, candidly claiming—as noted in Elizabeth Rosenthal's 2001 book *His Song: The Musical Journey of Elton John*—that Caribou is "a piece of crap. The sound is the worst, the songs are nowhere, the sleeve came out wrong, the lyrics weren't that good, the singing wasn't all there, the playing wasn't great, and the production is plain

lousy." Apart from that, one assumes, he thought it was OK. For all the self-deprecation, *Caribou* did come up with two jewels in the Elton John crown. The fluently orchestrated "Don't Let the Sun Go Down on Me," with backing vocals from Beach Boys Bruce Johnston and Carl Wilson and Toni Tenille, is an ocean-sized plea against emotional rejection that emphasized the serious side to Elton's music and has become one of his most loved ballads. While it first reached No. 2 in the US, its modest UK chart peak of No. 16 was eclipsed in 1991 when a live duet between Elton and George Michael (they'd first performed it together at Live Aid in 1985) swept it to No. 1 in both countries, giving it a second life.

"The Bitch Is Back" has also become a signifier and go-to phrase for Elton's career. The uncompromisingly rocky track, led by Johnstone's guitar riff, parodies the star's over-the-top lifestyle in its lyrics, though Taupin has agreed that his wife Maxine came up with the phrase, dropping it in when Elton would turn up in a grumpy mood. One Dusty Springfield contributed backing vocals. Amusingly, the word "bitch" was

In California during his 1974 US tour.

> Not only is [the song] one of Taupin's finest set of lyrics, Elton's vocal . . . convey[s] brilliantly the desperation and urgency of the words.

ROBERT HILBURN, *LOS ANGELES TIMES*, ON "DON'T LET THE SUN GO DOWN ON ME"

CARIBOU

TRACK LIST

SIDE ONE
The Bitch Is Back
Pinky
Grimsby
Dixie Lily
Solar Prestige a Gammon
You're So Static

SIDE TWO
I've Seen the Saucers
Stinker
Don't Let the Sun Go Down on Me
Ticking

Recorded at Caribou Ranch, Nederland, Colorado; Brother Studios, Santa Monica, California, USA; Trident Studios, London, England
Produced by Gus Dudgeon
Released June 28, 1974
Label DJM Records, DJLPH 439
Highest chart position on release
UK 1, US 1, CAN 1, AUS 1, ITA 8, JPN 2, SPA 4, GER 3, NOR 6

PERSONNEL
Elton John: vocals, piano, Hammond organ (9)
Davey Johnstone: acoustic guitar, electric guitar, mandolin, backing vocals
Dee Murray: bass guitar, backing vocals
Nigel Olsson: drums, backing vocals
Ray Cooper: tambourine, congas, whistle, vibraphone, snare, castanets, tubular bells, maracas
Bruce Johnston: backing vocals (9)
Carl Wilson: backing vocals (9)
Clydie King, Sherlie Matthews, Jessie Mae Smith, Dusty Springfield, Toni Tennille, Billy Hinsche: additional backing vocals
Tower of Power: horn section (1, 6, 8, 9)
David Hentschel: ARP, synthesizer (2, 5, 10; mellotron on (9)
Lenny Pickett: tenor saxophone (1), soprano saxophone (4, 5); clarinet (5)
Chester D. Thompson: Hammond organ (8)

COVER ART
David Larkham and Michael Ross: art direction and sleeve design

PREVIOUS PAGE: After a performance, London, 1974.
LEFT: Elton John celebrates the launch of his Elton John 1974 tour, Los Angeles.
BELOW: John Lennon plays his last concert, with Elton, at Madison Square Garden, November 28, 1974
RIGHT: Performing in London, 1974.

considered too risqué for radio play in some parts of the US. Elton has always enjoyed playing the song live, often to open his shows with a gust of energy. Tina Turner and Miley Cyrus are among those who've covered it.

From Dusty to Bolan to the British actress Nanette Newman, Elton was making a habit of bonding with fellow pop stars and celebrities, a trait he's continued with fervor to the modern day. In '74, he upped the ante on this, bonding with a former Beatle. His cover of "Lucy in the Sky with Diamonds," recorded at Caribou, featured backing vocals and guitar from John Lennon himself, under his pseudonym of Dr. Winston O'Boogie. The song Elton described as one of the best ever written gave him another US No. 1 in January 1975, and he emphasized his Lennon-love by covering "One Day (At a Time)" from *Mind Games* as the B-side, with Lennon on guitar. The new-best-friends bromance didn't end there, with Elton supplying backing vocals and piano on John's own chart-topper "Whatever Gets You Thru the Night." Lennon did pay a price, however. During the recording, Elton bet him it would go to No. 1. Lennon was the only ex-Beatle who hadn't had one of those at this stage, and, confident it wouldn't happen, agreed that he'd join Elton onstage if it did. And thus did a nervous to the point of throwing up beforehand Lennon, now a victim of stage fright, appear at Elton's Thanksgiving Day show at Madison Square Garden on November 28, 1974. The ovation lasted almost ten minutes. It was his last concert. Elton described it as "a joyous occasion," as the audience and even some of his band were overwhelmed by the combination of surprise and emotion. They played the aforementioned two hits plus "I Saw Her Standing There." "We're trying to think of a number to finish off with so I can run out of here and be sick," announced Lennon to the stunned crowd. "And we thought we'd do one by an old estranged flame of mine called Paul. This is one I never sang: we just about know how to play it." Elton had originally suggested they do "Imagine," but John had decreed that idea "boring." He later recalled "a great high night, a really high night. . . . I was moved by it but everybody else was in tears. I felt guilty that I wasn't."

The pair of pop legends spent plenty of time together, with the boy from Pinner pinching himself. He was peaking. Critics, though, were getting sniffy. He wasn't credible enough; he was too popular; he wasn't railing against The Man—worst of all, he appeared to enjoy fun. The stadium tours were according to some too lucrative, too soulless. And John Reid's aggressive streak was felt to be overbearing and arrogant in some quarters of the media. In Auckland, he was arrested for allegedly punching a female journalist in the face. Elton too was arrested for assaulting a friend of the journalist's who had made remarks that were construed as threatening (Elton had only grabbed the man's collar though; Reid had intervened and knocked the man over). Elton was not charged and asked to pay a small fee for court costs, but Reid was handed a twenty-eight day custodial sentence. Later there was talk of Reid's temper being out of control when drinking. Elton too was a heavy drinker in this period, but now, eventually with terrible consequences, he fell prey to the mysterious attraction of drugs. Reid, by his own admission, was taking plenty of cocaine. It isn't entirely surprising that Elton—and Bernie too—developed an addiction to the white stuff. It was almost ubiquitous in the rock world. Bernie's marriage to Maxine fell apart. None of this excuses the patchiness of *Caribou* but it does shed light on the group's prolific output and workaholic tendencies. Not that it thwarted the immense pleasure Elton drew—some distance away from Madison Square Garden—from playing a benefit show at Watford Football Club's Vicarage Road ground. The boyhood fan helped the then-small and struggling club, as he was shortly

to do to an even greater degree. His old pal Rod Stewart was happy to park any ego and serve as Elton's support act. They'd enjoyed a friendly rivalry for some years, since their John Baldry days, and had nicknames for each other. To Elton, Rod was Phyllis, and to Rod, Elton was Sharon. "Sharon" wrapped up an eventful '74 with a celebratory Hammersmith Odeon show, screened on BBC2 on *The Old Grey Whistle Test*.

The curveballs kept coming as Elton's first release of 1975 saw him luxuriating in the sound of Philly soul. "Philadelphia Freedom" was another US No. 1, created by John and Taupin at the request of Billie Jean King, Elton's latest celebrity pal and champion of feminist and LGBT rights, who played for the Philadelphia Freedoms team. Taupin stated that he couldn't write a song about tennis, and so did not. This hasn't stopped millions of listeners from hearing within it the patriotic pride they desire. It's become a state anthem. With Gene Page (Barry

LEFT: Elton, "Sharon", and Rod Stewart, "Phyllis", train with Watford Football Club, 1974.
RIGHT: Supporting tennis star Billie Jean King during Wimbledon, July 6, 1974.
BELOW: Celebrating his 27th birthday with footballers Martin Chivers (left) and Ian Morgan (second right) and friends, March 26, 1974.

ABOVE & RIGHT: Elton, in giant shoes, performs the song "Pinball Wizard" in the Who's rock opera movie *Tommy*, 1975.

White, the Supremes) in charge of the orchestral arrangement, the track is thoroughly convincing in its soul chops. (That live rendition of "I Saw Her Standing There" with Lennon made a covetable B-side).

Another one-off Elton single remains to this day the only cover of a song by the Who to reach the British Top 10. The spectacular, loud, and often orgiastic Ken Russell film of Pete Townshend's rock opera *Tommy* gave us Elton as the Pinball Wizard, resplendent and happily self-mocking in comedy specs, braces, and stilted sky-high boots. Driven again by Davey

Johnstone's guitar—he brought the rock to Elton's romping—it even throws in a cheeky reference to another Who song, "I Can't Explain."

Playing by intuition, Elton now made two career moves, one of which time has proven to be inspired and one that has proven to be folly. The latter involved dumping key members of his loyal band. The former led to an autobiographical album that stripped away the froth and glamour and gave the world intimate insight into Elton and Bernie's background and real selves. In theory it shouldn't have worked, showing us the levers behind the curtain in Oz. In fact, it gave us the finest Elton John album of all. *Captain Fantastic and the Brown Dirt Cowboy* revealed something of John's and Taupin's true identities, resulting in a record that, while dressed as an epic and fabulous concept work, shone with sensitivity and soul.

Bernie claims to have written the narrative songs in chronological order. They tell the sometimes romanticized, sometimes realistic tale of the writing couple's struggles in their early years in the music business in the late sixties, building to their eventual big breakthrough as the seventies swanned in. The album's booklet, with eye-catching artwork by Alan Aldridge, who'd worked with the Beatles and the Who, supported the lyrics in their candor, albeit with no little sense of self-dramatization. Elton has said that he wrote the music while on a journey by ship from England to New York, during which he had plenty of time for pause and reflection. He told *Almost Famous* director Cameron Crowe in 2006 that he'd always deemed *Captain Fantastic* "probably my finest album, because it wasn't commercial in any way. We did have songs such as 'Someone Saved My Life Tonight,' which is one of the best songs that Bernie and I have ever written together, but whether a [six-minute] song like that could be a single these days is questionable. [The album] was written from start to finish in running order, as a kind of story about coming to terms with failure—or trying desperately not to be one. We lived that story."

Importantly, the band took their time (by their standards) over this one, perhaps educated by the disappointing lack of focus of the rushed *Caribou* album. Yes, they spent less than a month on it, back at Caribou Ranch, but even that offered a chance to hone and polish which recent hit-and-run recording sessions hadn't. Gus Dudgeon thrived in the relatively relaxed pace, and also cited it as his favorite, declaring that there isn't one song on it that's "less than incredible." He'd pushed Elton to go bigger on the vocals on the outstanding track and centerpiece, which is undoubtedly "Someone Saved My Life

Tonight," where singer and musicians conjure up a swelling melodrama—musically inspired, Elton has said, by the Beach Boys' "God Only Knows"—too often absent in their more throwaway workouts. You could quibble on the poetic license taken with geography—Highbury doesn't truly count as "East End"—but there's a frankness and even fury to it. It covered that messy engagement to Linda Woodrow, towards whom, probably unfairly, some vicious couplets and acrimony are targeted, and Elton's ham-fisted suicide attempt of 1968. The "someone" of the story is Long John Baldry (also referenced as "Sugar Bear"), who'd talked Elton into calling off the marriage—the path not taken—and rescuing his musical career.

As the only single from the album, its lack of radio-friendliness (Elton wouldn't allow a shorter edit) meant it struggled in the UK, failing to make the Top 20. In the US, however, it triumphed, becoming the first single ever to enter the *Billboard* Hot 100 at No. 1. In *Rolling Stone*, writer and subsequent Springsteen seer Jon Landau insightfully posited that, "As long as Elton John can bring forth one performance per album in the order of [this], the chance remains that he will become something more than the great entertainer he already is and go on to make a lasting contribution to rock."

It's a pity this more portentous approach wasn't explored more often (though *Blue Moves* was to deliver some angst), as the reaction to the album proved his fans loved emotion as much as they enjoyed effervescence. It became the first album ever to go straight in at No. 1 on the *Billboard* chart, when released in May 1975. It sold a million and a half copies in its first four days, and stayed at the top for seven weeks. As an unabashedly autobiographical concept album, it still doesn't always receive its due credit. It was the last for many years to feature the classic lineup of his band (who, for now, went out on an artistic high): more on that soon. And Bernie is in his element, navel-gazing and impressionistically describing their difficult years, in an act of self-mythology that charms rather than irritates. Any songwriter essaying such indulgence nowadays would be laughed out of town, but in '75, an era of glam peacocks and spectacular self-aware showboating, it made sense. And so we're guided through the rise to fame of town mouse The Captain (Elton) and country mouse The Kid (Bernie), his busily scribbling, Western-fixated sidekick, as they battle to find the rent, (the Northwood Hills pub features on the sleeve). Taupin's tangle with reality may be narcissistic, but it draws out his most acute and affecting creations. John's chords are at their most moving on the double-whammy finale of "We All Fall in Love Sometimes" and "Curtains," which echo the grandeur of "Someone Saved My Life Tonight".

Elton told *Mojo* in 1997 that the former was "a beautiful love song, but not, as has been suggested elsewhere, about sexual love. . . . Bernie showed me things and ideas that I'd never

On top of the world, 1975.

encountered. He was the big brother I never had. In most ways we were so completely different, but . . . if he liked something, I thought there must be something in it. For instance, I'd listen to Dylan because Bernie thought he was the greatest writer ever . . . I hear "We All Fall in Love Sometimes" now and I can cry, because I remember the closeness that we had then."

There are sparkling pop songs herein too—"Bitter Fingers," "Better Off Dead," the sugar-coated country of "Writing," where Taupin tries to make even moving a pen across a sheet of paper sound like a Cecil B. DeMille–directed activity. Yet the overriding feeling one takes from this colorful, theatrical album is that it's the big artistic statement *Goodbye Yellow Brick Road* was touted as. It's extraordinary that a pop star on top of the world located the wherewithal to carve out such an openhearted classic. A reunited John and Taupin revisited and extended its themes with a kind of sequel in 2006's *The Captain and the Kid*, but by then the magical moment had been lost in the wind.

CAPTAIN FANTASTIC AND THE BROWN DIRT COWBOY

TRACK LIST

SIDE ONE
Captain Fantastic and the Brown Dirt Cowboy
Tower of Babel
Bitter Fingers
Tell Me When the Whistle Blows
Someone Saved My Life Tonight

SIDE TWO
(Gotta Get a) Meal Ticket
Better Off Dead
Writing
We All Fall in Love Sometimes
Curtains

Recorded at Caribou Ranch, Nederland, Colorado, USA
Produced by Gus Dudgeon
Released May 19, 1975
Label DJM Records, DJLPX 1
Highest chart position on release
UK 2, US 1, CAN 1, AUS 1, ITA 12, JPN 20, SPA 3, GER 22, NOR 2

PERSONNEL
Elton John: lead vocals, piano, Fender Rhodes, clavinet, mellotron, ARP, synthesizer, harpsichord
Davey Johnstone: acoustic guitar, electric and Leslie guitars; mandolin, piano on "Writing", backing vocals
Dee Murray: bass, backing vocals
Nigel Olsson: drums, backing vocals
Ray Cooper: shaker, congas, gong, jawbone, tambourine, bells, cymbals, triangle, bongos
David Hentschel: ARP, synthesizer (9, 10)
Gene Page: orchestral arrangement (4)

COVER ART
David Larkham and Bernie Taupin: art direction and graphic conception
Alan Aldridge: cover design

> "As long as Elton John can bring forth one performance per album in the order of [this], the chance remains that he will become something more than the great entertainer he already is and go on to make a lasting contribution to rock."

JON LANDAU, *ROLLING STONE*

Performing at Dodger Stadium in Los Angeles, October 26, 1975, wearing a sequinned baseball uniform.

> Bernie showed me things and ideas that I'd never encountered. He was the big brother I never had.
>
> ELTON JOHN

It was a swansong for the Elton John Band per se. Dee Murray and Nigel Olsson, the rhythm section who'd formed so much of the singer's signature sound, were now let go, while guitarist Johnstone remained in place for a couple more years. The classic lineup wouldn't record an album together again until 1983. Caleb Quaye and Roger Pope were brought back into the fold, and Kenny Passarelli became the new bass player. James Newton Howard, later a multiple Oscar nominee, joined the outfit in their studio work as a keyboardist and string arranger. The new band were introduced to the public at a sold-out Wembley Stadium show in June.

Elton later admitted his personnel reshuffle was "inexplicable." "I can't really understand why I did it," he told Johnnie Walker in 2005. "In retrospect . . . it was me trying to change things musically." Olsson has said there was much resentment, and that he got a call from Steve Brown announcing, "Elton doesn't want you guys involved in gigs or recording any more." Contemporaneous reports suggest he wanted a harder, heavier rock sound. This live direction though was confused by the classical musician Howard's involvement in recording. And almost everything was confused

by the lashings of cocaine flying around. The Wembley show was dreamed up as a triumphant homecoming, but Elton's decision to premiere the *Captain Fantastic* album in full didn't lead to sing-along crowd euphoria. Support act the Beach Boys had lifted everybody up on a sunny afternoon; Elton's new album brought everyone down in the evening. No matter: a month later he was joining the Rolling Stones onstage in Colorado, introduced by Mick Jagger, presumably to Elton's mild annoyance, as "Reg from Watford."

Reg from Watford promptly bought himself a thirty-seven-acre country estate close to Windsor Great Park, which meant he was almost literally rubbing shoulders with royalty. The absurd work-hard, play-hard ethic drove on, with another album, his tenth already, out just five months after *Captain Fantastic*. It was his last for the DJM label (partially explaining the crazed prolific output of recent years), fulfilling that deal, so now he could move to his own Rocket company. Free at last! *Rock of the Westies* duly became the second album in history to debut at No. 1 in the US, with the jaunty, Caribbean-tinged "Island Girl" (the lyrics of which, concerning a prostitute, seem problematic to

present-day ears) its attendant No. 1 single. (Again, both album and single performed less dazzlingly in Elton's homeland.) The new band was showcased, and Patti LaBelle and Kiki Dee contributed backing vocals. Throughout several lurches in tone and genre, as if the new band were all getting to know each other while mirroring the American funk-rock sounds of, say, Little Feat or the Doobie Brothers, perhaps the Eagles, Bernie maintains his comic-book obsessions on tracks like "I Feel Like a Bullet (In the Gun of Robert Ford)" and "Dan Dare (Pilot of the Future)." "Grow Some Funk of Your Own," with the band getting off on getting heavier, was a moderate US hit but the first single in five years to flop outside the Top 50 in Britain. Overall it felt as if Elton, whoever was in his band, had regressed from the courage of *Captain Fantastic* and found a comfort zone in the formula used on *Caribou*.

LEFT: At Caribou Ranch, Colorado, for the recording of his tenth album *Rock of the Westies*, 1974.
BELOW: Stage boots made for Elton John, 1974.

ROCK OF THE WESTIES

TRACK LIST

SIDE ONE
Medley (Yell Help / Wednesday Night / Ugly)
Dan Dare (Pilot of the Future)
Island Girl
Grow Some Funk of Your Own
I Feel Like a Bullet (In the Gun of Robert Ford)

SIDE TWO
Street Kids
Hard Luck Story
Feed Me
Billy Bones and the White Bird

Recorded at Caribou Ranch, Nederland, Colorado, USA
Produced by Gus Dudgeon
Released October 24, 1975
Label DJM Records, DJLPH 464
Highest chart position on release UK 5, US 1, CAN 1, AUS 4, FRA 5, ITA 16, JPN 47, SPA 8, GER 33, NOR 6

KEY PERSONNEL
Elton John: piano (all except 8), vocals
James Newton-Howard: harpsichord (1), ELKA Rhapsody string synthesizer (1), ARP synthesizer (1, 3), Hohner clavinet (1, 2), mellotron (3), electric piano (4, 5, 7, 8, 9), synthesizer (4, 5, 9)
Davey Johnstone: electric guitar (1, 3, 4, 5, 7, 8, 9), backing vocals (2, 3, 4, 6, 8), rhythm guitar (2, 6), voice bag (2), Ovation guitar (3), banjo (3), slide guitar (3, 6), acoustic guitar (4, 5), guitar solo (5)
Caleb Quaye: electric guitar (1, 2, 4, 5, 7, 8, 9), backing vocals (2, 3, 4, 6, 7, 8), acoustic guitar (3, 4, 5), rhythm guitar (6), lead guitar solo (6)
Kenny Passarelli: bass guitar, backing vocals (2, 3, 4, 6, 7)
Ray Cooper: tambourine (1, 3, 5, 6, 9), cowbell (1, 9), congas (1, 3, 6, 7, 8), jawbone (1), marimba (3), castanets (4), bell tree (4), vibraphone (4, 5, 8), shaker (8), wind chimes (8), maracas (9), kettle drums (9)

COVER ART
David Larkham: art direction and design
Terry O'Neill: album cover photograph

> # Already the most commercially successful solo rock act since Elvis, Elton John continues to grow in popularity and there's no end in sight.

ROLLING STONE

Success didn't seem to care what albums he put out. Los Angeles' mayor declared it Elton John Week as the singer played sell-out shows at the Dodger Stadium in glammed-up baseball gear and showed up for the unveiling of a star in his honor on Hollywood Boulevard. Soon he decided to live in L.A. for a while, encouraged by Reid, with tax issues and his massive American earnings in mind. Glamorously, he purchased a Beverly Hills mansion once owned by Greta Garbo. Less glamorously, his flesh was being tempted by the devil of drug addiction.

L.A. in the seventies was not short of cocaine users. Neither was its music business scene. Neither was Elton's extended entourage. His demeanor around this period has been described as anxious, niggly, stressed. A Russell Harty interview for ITV showed him looking out of it, his eyes wandering, his voice a muttering ramble, tailing off, toying with tangents then giving up the ghost. His new house was in a sense haunted. One day, he's said, he took an excess of sedatives and dove into his indoor pool. With the levity of hindsight, he's claimed he shouted that he'd be dead within hours and that his granny responded that the visitors might as well depart then. He was in a coma for around forty-eight hours. In the 1996 documentary *Tantrums & Tiaras*, his mother recalled how distressing it was to see her beloved son so unhappy at the time, for all his surface success and global fame. She blamed his falling in with a bad crowd. "There were drugs, which he denied frantically," said Sheila, bursting into tears, "but I'm not daft." She added, "And that was only the start of it."

Unveiling his star on the Hollywood Walk of Fame, October 23, 1975.

The costumes had got wilder, the trademark spectacles zanier, the image more cartoonishly buoyant, but behind the painted smile Elton was wrestling with the demons of exhaustion and self-doubt. Over the first six years of the seventies he'd rattled through over five hundred shows across the world, recorded and released a dozen albums, and taken a beating from irregular hours, air miles, and a diet that certainly wasn't healthy enough to counter the drink and drugs. And then there was the inevitable dizzying effect that soaring celebrity can have on the mind and the ego, the sense of self, of identity. Depression dug in. While he kept any mention of drugs out of interviews, he began to muse to reporters that he was thinking of packing in his roller-coaster career, or at least the savagely fatiguing traveling and touring. Bernie, meanwhile, was drinking like a fish, and reported to be grumpy. This was a time of blue moves.

It was also a time of coming out, of buying his favorite football club, of landing his first UK No. 1 single with Kiki Dee, and of appearing jovially on *The Morecambe and Wise Show*. Elton John may have been downhearted, but he wouldn't be broken. In the seventies his life didn't know the meaning of a dull moment.

LEFT: Wearing a floral appliqué suit and sunglasses, 1975.
BELOW RIGHT: Cher and Elton, *The Cher Show*, 1975.
BELOW: Elton performs in concert, London, 1975.

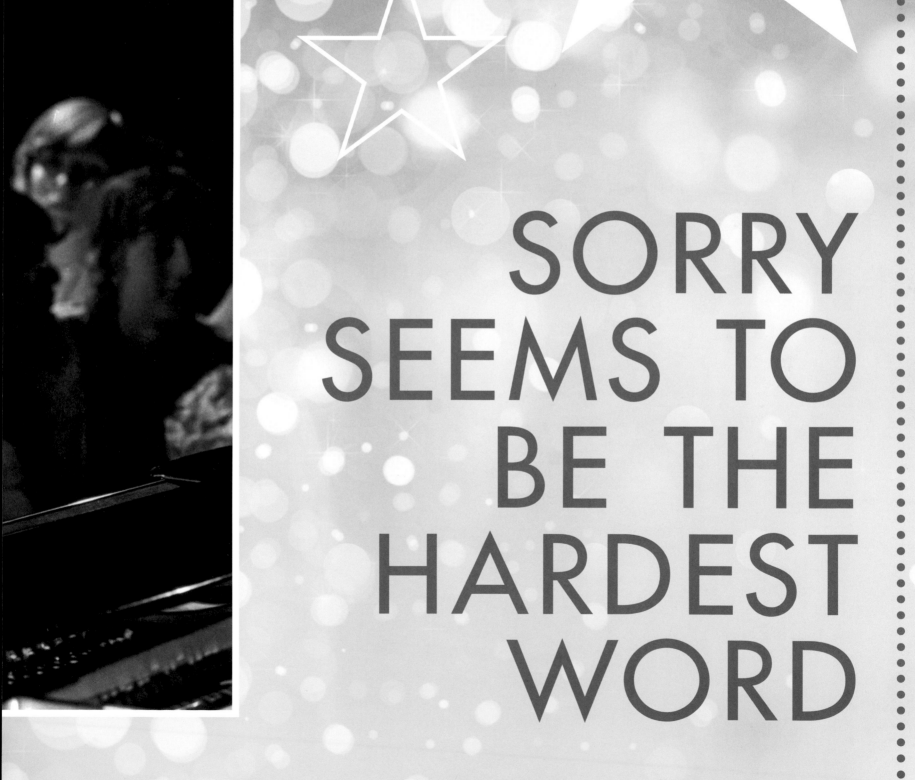

6

SORRY SEEMS TO BE THE HARDEST WORD

"We had tried to change with every album up to that point . . . I was aware that we had been at the peak of our careers, and that that was going to level off, and we just did a blatantly uncommercial album . . . *Blue Moves* is a very poignant album. We were all weary, feeling the pressure and needed a break. Out of those situations comes rawness, and some of the lyrics are desperate. I just love the album.

ELTON JOHN

lton John had of late appeared onstage wearing $5,000 glasses which spelled his name out in lights, a Statue of Liberty costume, a Donald Duck costume, a Mozart costume, and multiple ostrich feathers. Reasonably, he began to worry that critics were no longer taking him seriously. He was seething in private, and sometimes in public. He was somewhat mollified when in August 1975, the inaugural Rock Music Awards in Santa Monica named him the outstanding rock personality of the year. He played four shows in two nights at the Troubadour in L.A. to mark five years since his breakthrough American debut there. He also appeared on *Soul Train*, one of the first few white artists to do so, which boosted his satisfaction and pride levels.

There was also a massive British hit single in the summer of '76, which killed off the jinx whereby he'd never had a No. 1 in his homeland. Even now it was an honor he had to share with good friend Kiki Dee, as the pair duetted on the upbeat, disco-tinged Motown pastiche "Don't Go Breaking My Heart." Gus Dudgeon again displayed his versatility as a producer, and Elton even chipped in with a few lyrics among Bernie's rough draft. James Newton Howard's swirling strings were a prominent feature, and a video of Elton and Kiki larking around on microphone as they sang it backed up the song's feelgood factor on what was an international crossover hit. As writers, John and Taupin here used the pseudonyms Ann Orson/Carte Blanche. (Dusty Springfield had at one point been mooted to accompany Elton on it). The song, which took the Ivor Novello Award for the year's best, remained Elton's only UK No. 1 for another fourteen years, and his last US No. 1 for twenty-one years. In '77, at the height of punk, he performed it with Miss Piggy on *The Muppet Show*.

PREVIOUS PAGE: Performing in Munich, Germany, February, 1976.
LEFT: Elton and Kiki Dee celebrate their chart success, 1976.

HERE AND THERE

TRACK LIST

SIDE ONE
Live in London at the Royal Festival Hall
Skyline Pigeon
Border Song
Honky Cat
Love Song
Crocodile Rock

SIDE TWO
Live in New York at Madison Square Garden
Funeral for a Friend / Love Lies Bleeding
Rocket Man
Bennie and the Jets
Take Me to the Pilot

Recorded at the Royal Festival Hall, London, England; Madison Square Garden, New York City, USA
Produced by Gus Dudgeon
Released April 30, 1976
Label DJM Records, DJLPH 473
Highest chart position on release US 4

PERSONNEL

Elton John: piano, vocals
Ray Cooper: percussion
Davey Johnstone: guitars, background vocals
Dee Murray: bass, background vocals
Nigel Olsson: drums, background vocals

COVER ART

David Larkham: art direction and design

NOTES

The album was at the time issued in part to fulfill a final contractual obligation John owed to DJM Records, prior to having his records released by his own Rocket Record Company label, starting with *Blue Moves* in 1976.

While the single gave the Rocket label its first statement smash, it transpired that one more Elton release was required to wrap up contractual obligations with DJM, who had dealt such a canny hand at the outset of his career. *Here and There*, released in April '76, was a live album put together to take care of this. It gathered recordings from two 1974 shows, "here" being the Royal Festival Hall, on side one, and "there" being Madison Square Garden, on side two. It felt a little perfunctory, and reviews reflected this. For a 1995 reissue, Dudgeon remixed and expanded the sets to greater effect.

Next came another double album. Recorded in March in Toronto, London, Los Angeles, and Santa Monica—indicating a lack of cohesion brought on by the exhausting touring commitments—*Blue Moves*, released October '76, is an outlier among Elton's catalog. Initially unloved by both critics and fans, it's grown in stature since, as ears warm to the overriding moody, introspective flavor, which turned many people off at that time. The lukewarm reception hit hard, especially as it was Elton's first release on his and Reid's Rocket. Yes, the singer was running out of creative stamina after a preposterously prolific few years under the spotlight, but there was an intriguing romantic melancholy to the album's atmosphere, as if he and Taupin had taken the more forlorn elements of *Captain Fantastic*

LEFT: Singing "Crocodile Rock" on *The Muppet Show*, 1977.
ABOVE: With Miss Piggy, duetting on "Don't Go Breaking My Heart", 1977.

BLUE MOVES

TRACK LIST

SIDE ONE
Your Starter for . . .
Tonight
One Horse Town
Chameleon

SIDE TWO
Boogie Pilgrim
Cage the Songbird
Crazy Water
Shoulder Holster

SIDE THREE
Sorry Seems to be the
    Hardest Word
Out of the Blue
Between Seventeen and Twenty
The Wide-Eyed and Laughing
Someone's Final Song

SIDE FOUR
Where's the Shoorah?
If There's a God in Heaven
    (What's He Waiting For?)
Idol
Theme from a Non-existent TV Series
Bite Your Lip (Get Up and Dance!)

Recorded at Eastern Sound, Toronto, Canada; Abbey Road Studios, London, England; Sunset Sound, Los Angeles; Brother Studios, Santa Monica, USA
Produced by Gus Dudgeon
Released October 22, 1976
Label The Rocket Record Company, OSP 1, OC
Highest chart position on release UK 3, US 3, CAN 4, AUS 8, FRA 6, ITA 9, JPN 53, SPA 10, GER 39, NOR 5

KEY PERSONNEL
Elton John: piano (1–5, 7–10, 13–16, 18), vocals (2–9, 12–16, 18), vocalese (11), harmonium (14), harpsichord (17)
Paul Buckmaster: string arrangements and conductor (3, 7, 15), brass arrangements (7)
Davey Johnstone: mandolin (2, 11, 17), electric guitar (3, 7, 10, 15), slide guitar (5, 18), acoustic guitar (6), dulcimer (6), sitar (12), slide guitar (18)
James Newton-Howard: synthesizer (1, 3, 6, 10, 12, 13, 17, 18), piano, Fender Rhodes (3, 9, 13, 17), Hammond organ (5, 11, 15), mellotron (6), clavinet (7)
Kenny Passarelli: bass guitar (1, 3, 4, 5, 7–11, 14–18)
Roger Pope: drums (1, 3, 4, 5, 7, 8, 10, 11, 15–18)
Caleb Quaye: acoustic guitar (1, 4, 6, 12, 17), electric guitar (3, 4, 7, 10, 11, 15, 18), guitar solo (3, 10, 15), twelve-string guitar (12)

COVER ART
David Costa: art direction and coordination
David Nutter: photography
Patrick Procktor: painting

> **Every artist comes to a crossroads. Who wants to be a 45-year-old entertainer in Vegas like Elvis?**
>
> ELTON JOHN

RIGHT: Bernie and Elton at Studio 54, New York City, 1978.

and decided to delve into them further. It wasn't as simple as that: much of the mood is built by James Newton Howard's unapologetically florid keyboards and orchestral arrangements. Yet there is an innate poignancy to much of this, as if those concerned knew it marked the demise of an era. Which it did, being the last John-Taupin collaboration of their first period of flowering. Most would agree that, though they were to reconvene some years on, their bond was never to be quite the same. The ceaseless touring, too, was soon to take a serious and necessary pause, and after *Blue Moves*, the band, who again excel on it, were sadly shorn of Pasarelli, Pope, and Quaye. Equally if not more significantly, it was the last Elton John album to be produced by Gus Dudgeon for over a decade.

However, let's not forget that Elton's popularity was still immense. For all of its downbeat tropes, *Blue Moves* went top three in both the US and UK, going gold. As was the case with *Captain Fantastic*, one wonders if this was a musical area—or mood-board—that a more daring artist could have continued to

journey into with fruitful results. And indeed, Elton has with hindsight declared it another of his favorites.

As a double, it's the inverse of the mostly frolicsome *Goodbye Yellow Brick Road*. The *Village Voice* called it "impossibly weepy" and "excessive," while *Rolling Stone* thought the long instrumental passages (often conceived by Howard) were indulgent at "the exclusion of sense." Perhaps the cover artwork, from Patrick Procktor's painting *The Guardian Readers*, revealed that Elton did harbor a desire to be taken more seriously than the wacky glasses and outfits might suggest. "Sorry Seems to Be the Hardest Word" was the sole hit, while "Tonight" (with the London Symphony Orchestra, conducted by Howard), "Idol," and "Cage the Songbird" were equally pensive in tone, the latter allowing Bernie to ponder the life of Edith Piaf instead of Marilyn. "Between Seventeen and Twenty" shows off Bernie's craving for the innocence of youth again. "Someone's Final Song" appears to concern a writer, drinking, contemplating suicide. This was the first

album where Elton had looked at some of Bernie's lyrics and said he couldn't sing them.

On the other hand, "One Horse Town" (which Elton in later years rebooted as a set opener) and "Bite Your Lip (Get Up and Dance)" eschew the introversion, embracing R&B, while the gospel-tinged "Boogie Pilgrim" brings in grandstanding choirs. The lively and inventive instrumental "Out of the Blue" is more than a little prog. "Chameleon," an intricate slow-burner which develops real momentum, featured Beach Boy Bruce Johnston and Toni Tenille on backing vocals, even though the Beach Boys had declined Elton's offering of the song to them two years earlier. Among other big names flitting in for cameos were David Crosby and Graham Nash, the Brecker Brothers, David Sanborn, and one Paul Buckmaster, still very much on the Dudgeon radar. And more subtly effective than Howard, who on his learning curve had a tendency towards bombast.

As his first album in seven not to grab an obligatory American No. 1, *Blue Moves* was a strange candidate to be Elton's first

to reach platinum status, but this it did—partly because such certification didn't exist until '76. Plaintive evergreen ballad "Sorry Seems to Be the Hardest Word" has survived a 2002 duet with boy band Blue (which got to No. 1 in Britain, eleven places higher than Elton's original) and being employed in a 2015 US cat food ad.

Bernie Taupin has talked about the album being another penned under the usual pressure to deliver monster success, with "a feeling of how many times can we keep doing this?" Elton has mused, "We'd tried to change with every album up to that point, but this was the most drastic. I was aware that we had been at the peak of our careers, and that that was going to level off. And we just did a blatantly uncommercial album. It wasn't on purpose—it's full of fine songs and has a great band. I think *Blue Moves* is . . . very poignant. We were all weary, needing a break. Out of those situations comes rawness, and some of the lyrics are desperate. I just love the album." He's admitted to listening to 10cc's "I'm Not in Love" "everywhere—in the car, at home—I'd sob like a baby" while making the record.

It proved a watershed. "Every artist comes to a crossroads," said Elton. And with a hostage-to-fortune quip of "Who wants to be a 45-year-old entertainer in Vegas like Elvis?" he stunned fans by announcing his retirement from touring (or at least, he told *Rolling Stone*, it was "highly unlikely" he'd tour again). From the vantage point of the twenty-first century, his declaration seems premature, but he was aware he was burning out and knew it was "time to cool it." There had been few gigs to promote *Blue Moves*. At last, after the years of relentless hurried sessions, there was a two-year gap until the next album. During a Wembley Arena charity show in '77, Captain Fantastic stated—with a hint of drama à la Bowie's infamous Ziggy Stardust "Retirement Gig" in July 1973— "I haven't been touring for a long time. It's been a painful decision whether to come back on the road or not . . . and I've made a decision tonight. This is going to be the last show. There's a lot more to me than playing on the road."

Some of this "more" was beginning to emerge. In two on-paper contrasting gambits, he came out regarding his sexuality, and his relationship with Watford Football Club kicked on to a new level. In October '76 he told a *Rolling Stone* interviewer that he was bisexual (he didn't completely come out as gay until the late eighties). The same year, he became chairman and director of the football club he'd supported growing up in nearby Pinner.

The *Rolling Stone* "confessional" bore the heading "Elton's Frank Talk—The Lonely Love Life of a Superstar." Elton spoke

candidly of depression, bad moods, and the contrast between his "Disney film" public life and his private dissatisfaction. His relationship with John Reid was winding down (they remained close). He said, telling the interviewer to keep the tape running, "I've never talked about this before . . . there's nothing wrong with going to bed with somebody of your own sex. I think everybody's bisexual to a certain degree. I don't think it's just me. It's not a bad thing to be. I think you're bisexual. I think everybody is." While Bowie had broken taboos in Britain, much of America wasn't quite ready for this. There were letters of protest, but Elton figured it wasn't as big a deal as some suggested. He even told *Sounds* later in the year that it was a big anticlimax. "More people wave to me than before, that's all. Nobody seems to harbor a grudge against me. Especially within the football club. Although there has been a bit of shouting from the terraces." By coincidence or not, Elton's commercial wobble started here. Friends have said that he resented Bowie for cornering the market in gay mystique even though he was predominantly straight, whereas he had felt he had to play straight even though he was gay. While Elton now toned down his outfits a little, feeling he'd have more credibility without the cartoonish over-the-top

LEFT: Elton and his pet rabbit Clarence pose for a portrait at his home near London, 1976.
ABOVE RIGHT: Wembley, 1977: Would it be Elton's last concert?

"After fourteen albums we needed a break from each other."

ELTON JOHN

wardrobe choices, he was still prone to maneuvers like wearing a giant gold banana around his middle regions.

That sense of humor helped him bat off homophobic chants from seventies' football crowds. As chairman of Watford, he got plenty of practice as opposition fans worked their vocal cords. He'd first bought shares in his favored club in 1973, was invited to invest and given the title of vice president. But he wasn't an absentee supporter: he'd attend matches whenever geography allowed, and plugged the club not only in interviews but in the video for "Step into Christmas." For the then-small club, this was major publicity. A year on, he was a director, and plowing more backing into the Hornets, who were languishing in the old Fourth Division (the bottom league). When Elton was elected chairman in '76, he used the time out he'd allowed himself from music (apart from enjoying Rocket Records' success) to throw himself into helping them rise. He got John Reid in as another investor, and became engrossed in his new mission. Reid and he had by then split, and the manager had moved out of the Hercules home, but his business empire thrived, including a brief spell managing Queen. The music world's money boosted Watford's hopes, and when Elton appointed Graham Taylor as manager there began a joyful period in their history. Grounded Lincolnshire man Taylor seemed as different to the singer as two men could be, but they formed an unlikely bond as the football club's fortunes soared.

They marched unstoppably up to the First Division, peaking when they finished runners-up to Liverpool in 1983. A year later they made the FA Cup Final, losing to Everton. Such heights had seemed unthinkable before Elton's (and subsequent England manager Taylor's) time. Elton sold the club in 1987, retaining the title of president, but bought it back a decade later. He's remained involved at various levels since (as they enjoy another healthy period in the big-money Premier League present day, he still holds financial interests), and in 2014 the boyhood fan was at Vicarage Road stadium to witness the opening of the Elton John Stand. "One of the greatest days of my life," he said proudly.

Musically, a fallow period was taking place, rest and recuperation necessary not just for Elton but for Bernie, the band, and the whole crew. Gus Dudgeon, producer of every album bar *Empty Sky*, left after a dispute over money, though Elton told *Sounds* that also "after fourteen albums we needed a break from each other. Also, by now I know exactly what I want." Dudgeon reckoned he fell out with Rocket Records, not Elton. He felt the label was losing momentum, and that getting Elton, Bernie, and John Reid to sit down in the same room,

LEFT: Live with giant golden banana hanging from a chain, 1977.
RIGHT: The proud chairman of Watford Football Club, 1977.

never mind discuss policy, was too difficult. Others have opined that Gus's iron rule in the studio was by now too controlling for Elton, who'd come a long way from the young, eager wannabe Dudgeon had honed into a marketable star. The producer would go on to work with Joan Armatrading, Gilbert O'Sullivan, the Beach Boys, and others, before reconvening with Elton much later. After he and his wife died in a car accident in 2002, Elton dedicated the *Peachtree Road* album to them.

Yet perhaps an even more seismic shock to the successful Elton John formula was his split with Bernie Taupin. After close to a decade of working in union, and growing up in public together as fast friends, there had evolved a mutual awareness that it was time to give each other what's commonly known as some space. The singer, who encouraged Bernie, with his blessing, to work with others (he wrote for Alice Cooper's album *From the Inside*), sensed they had been getting a little worn and weary as a creative pair. He told one interviewer that he'd made too many albums "in the same key," and that the rapport he and Bernie had at first was growing stale. Since the young days of sharing a flat and listening to records together they'd drifted,

with writing since *Honky Château* becoming something they did, often via the post, without physically meeting (with the exception of *Captain Fantastic*, which might explain its superior emotional timbre). Bernie had indisputably changed from his innocent days as a country lad. Living in L.A., moping over the failure of his marriage, he was drinking heavily, almost like a parody of the characters on *Blue Moves*. His doctors advised him to clean up his act. He decamped to Acapulco for a period of detox. The old days of Elton and Bernie dreaming of glory under Pinner skies were long gone.

Was a thirty-year-old Elton John ideally placed to ride the wave of punk rock, the new era's defining movement? Possibly not. When, hating his baldness, he opted for a hair transplant, which the UK newspapers gleefully covered, he was not exactly perceived as the coolest thing by a generation enjoying the raucous rebellion of the Sex Pistols and the Clash. He spoke of the era as "brilliant," but his record sales plummeted, and his star was in the freezer. It was very fashionable to knock the old guard: the Eltons, Stones, Zeppelins, prog bands. Tough times for Captain Fantastic, so recently so unassailable. Luckily for

him, the punk "cleansing" was much more of a talking point in the UK than in America, where it had only cosmetic net effect.

Nonetheless, after the taxing schedule of the upward years, and despite a run of six early summer charity shows at London's Rainbow Theatre, he was learning to relate to "normal" life again, albeit with a tendency to excessive consumption of brandy. "I was being locked away like a prize tiger," he told *Sounds.* "Royalty probably weren't treated as well as I've been for the last few years." He added, "I know it's boring, but being involved in the soccer club has brought me down to Earth. Mixing with the same people who used to go to the [Northwood Hills] pub I played in when I was 17 or 18 . . ." He'd still turn up to Watford FC in outrageous clothes. This led Graham Taylor to discipline the players if they stepped out of line with the tongue-in-cheek comment that he had enough on his hands teaching Elton John how to be a football club chairman. The chairman was at the same time helping a band to a hit with Rocket Records. The song was "Gonna Capture Your Heart," and the band was Blue—but not the boy band of the same name he'd later collaborate with. As for his own music, he indulged his

love of Philly soul by working in Sigma Sound in Philadelphia with Thom Bell, the man behind the sound of the Stylistics, Delfonics, and other greats. The resulting tracks stayed on file awhile, though one—"Are You Ready for Love?"—was to prove a surprise comeback No. 1 a quarter of a century later. Bell had enough backbone to advise Elton to sing in a lower register, a device that was to give him vocal longevity.

Another song they worked on there was his first full co-write with Gary Osborne, "Shine on Through." Osborne was to take Taupin's role as lyricist for the next Elton John album, and intermittently thereafter. They'd been friends for some time, and after Elton asked him to come up with something for a piano melody, Osborne seized the day. While there are few who believe Osborne ever usurped Taupin in fans' affections, he did help Elton get back on the horse, as it were, bringing him sunshine. Their teaming-up was debuted by Elton on the 1977 Morecambe and Wise Christmas special. Just to place this in perspective: it was watched by 28 million people, over half the British population. Elton proved a good sport, pretending to get lost in the BBC studio complex as Eric and Ernie gently mocked

FAR LEFT: A mountainous pile of fan mail, Los Angeles, 1977. **LEFT:** In the dressing rooms at Watford Football Club, 1977.

> ## It's about the silliness of rock 'n' roll stars... it turned out to be one of the most sincere songs we've written.

ELTON JOHN

him. "I'm Elton John!" "Oh, sorry about that." Much like Des O'Connor, he eventually gets to sing his song. Afterwards, he sighs, "That's what I was going to do on *The Morecambe and Wise Show* . . ." "It's a good job you didn't!" chirps Eric, dressed as a cleaning lady.

Affable chuckles all round, but behind the scenes Elton was somewhat chastened, his Hollywood lifestyle and celebrity circle diminished (how soon they forget) and his addictions clambering in again. Cocaine and brandy were the dominant demons. Gary Osborne told biographer David Buckley that his new colleague was forsaking sleep, drinking to counter the coke. His first album since the breakup with Bernie and Gus, *A Single Man*, was put together under the yoke of such addictions. Cocaine is notoriously a drug that convinces you that all your ideas are genius. Unsurprisingly, most of them aren't. A prelude single, "Ego," ultimately left off the album, was a swansong John-Taupin composition, a leftover from *Blue Moves* that boasted peculiar tempos and an expensive video. It flopped. "'Ego' was just something I had lying around," explained Elton. "Unfortunately, the time wasn't right. It's been disappointing. [Bernie and] I never thought of it as an autobiography until it came out. It's about the silliness of rock 'n' roll stars, and the video was supposed to show how stupid rock 'n' roll can be. The grotesque side of rock 'n' roll. And it turned out to be one of the most sincere songs we've ever written."

Now it was up to Osborne to provide any lyrical sincerity, or irony, or any points between. If Dudgeon wasn't producing (bassist Clive Franks was brought in for that role, though reluctant to follow Dudgeon's tough act), Elton nonetheless

Reading fan mail, Hilversum, Netherlands, 1978.

A SINGLE MAN

TRACK LIST

SIDE ONE
Shine on Through
Return to Paradise
I Don't Care
Big Dipper
It Ain't Gonna Be Easy

SIDE TWO
Part Time Love
Georgia
Shooting Star
Madness
Reverie
Song for Guy

Recorded at the Mill, Cookham, Berkshire, England
Produced by Clive Franks & Elton John
Released October 16, 1978
Label The Rocket Record Company, TRAIN 1
Highest chart position on release UK 8, US 15, CAN 12, AUS 8, FRA 2, ITA 13, JPN 74, SPA 12, GER 17, NOR 4

KEY PERSONNEL

Elton John: lead vocals, backing vocals (1, 2, 8), pianos (1, 4, 11), piano (2, 3, 5, 6, 7, 9, 10), clavinet (3), harmonium (7), church organ (7), Fender Rhodes (8), mellotron (11), Polymoog (11), Solina String synthesizer (11)
Ray Cooper: tambourine (1, 3-7, 9), marimba (2), shakers (2, 8, 11), vibraphone (5), congas (6, 9), tympani (9), wind chimes (11), rhythm box (11)
Paul Buckmaster: orchestra arrangements (1, 3, 5, 6, 9), arrangements (2), ARP synthesizer (10)
Clive Franks: bass guitar (1-7, 9, 11)
Tim Renwick: acoustic guitar (2, 3), electric guitar (4, 5, 6, 9), Leslie guitar (7), mandolin (7)

COVER ART

David Costa: sleeve design
Mike Storey: graphic design
Terry O'Neill: photography

NOTES

A Single Man was the first album where Gary Osborne replaced Bernie Taupin as lyricist. It is also the only Elton John album to not have any tracks co-written by Bernie Taupin on the original cut.

elected to record at Gus's brand-new studio, the Mill, in Cookham, Berkshire, over the first three quarters of '78. Changes continued: this was the last album to involve Paul Buckmaster for many years, and while Ray Cooper was still present, Davey Johnstone only played on first single "Part Time Love." Elton, singing from now on in the lower register Thom Bell had recommended, wrote his melodies first and the lyrics were then fitted in by Osborne. On the cover, Elton, photographed in Windsor Great Park near his home, looked the very opposite of the colorful, flamboyant character traditionally associated with him. Dressed in funereal black, sporting a top hat and cane, the shot won a *Music Week* award but didn't endear itself to record buyers missing their upbeat Elton fix.

Released in October, the album sold respectably but not tremendously. The presence of "Watford Football Club" on

backing vocals on two tracks may or may not have helped. The two contrasting singles each had merit; "Part Time Love" had a soulful swing, while "Song for Guy," effectively an instrumental penned solely by Elton, was a tribute to a teenage Rocket Records messenger boy, Guy Burchett, killed in a motorcycle accident. Elton's liner notes gave some insight into his mordant moods at this time: "As I was writing this song one Sunday, I imagined myself floating into space and looking down at my own body. I was imagining myself dying. Morbidly obsessed with these thoughts, I wrote this song about death. The next day I was told that Guy . . . had been tragically killed, on the day

LEFT: Still dressing to impress, Windsor, England, 1978.
BELOW: During his Russia tour, May 1979.

VICTIM OF LOVE

TRACK LIST

SIDE ONE
Johnny B. Goode
Warm Love in a Cold World
Born Bad

SIDE TWO
Thunder in the Night
Spotlight
Street Boogie
Victim of Love

Recorded at Musicland Studios, Munich, Germany; Rusk Sound Studios, Hollywood, USA
Produced by Pete Bellotte
Released October 13, 1979
Label The Rocket Record Company, HISPD 125
Highest chart position on release UK 41, US 35, CAN 28, AUS 20, NOR 18

KEY PERSONNEL

Elton John: lead and backing vocals
Thor Baldursson: keyboards, arrangements
Tim Cansfield: rhythm guitar
Paulinho Da Costa: percussion
Roy Davies: keyboards
Keith Forsey: drums
Marcus Miller: bass guitar
Craig Snyder: lead guitar

COVER ART

David Bailey: photography
Jubilee Graphics: design

NOTES

At under 36 minutes, the album is the shortest of Elton John's career, and is atypical of his recording career in several respects. He neither wrote the songs nor played piano or keyboards, only providing the vocals. It was his first album without any of his original band members.

I wrote the song." The only words, floating in towards the end, are "Life isn't everything."

Life wasn't as morose as Elton's mood swings may have depicted. He picked up touring again, becoming one of the first Western artists to tour the Soviet Union and Israel, accompanied just by Ray Cooper. One of his kept-on-ice Thom Bell tracks, "Mama Can't Buy You Love," took him back into the US Top 10, and a three-track EP emerged, though the potential of its eight-minute B-side, "Are You Ready for Love," wasn't yet noticed. Yet if this persuaded Elton that dance music was the way forward—and indeed the era of disco as king had not only arrived but had plateaued, meaning some bandwagon-hopping big stars had all but missed the boat—his next album was a thoroughly misguided misfire. *Victim of Love* (released October 1979) was panned by critics ("thoroughly objectionable," said *Melody Maker*) and one of his lowest-charting albums.

In theory it might have worked. Produced by Pete Bellotte, the Barnet-born, Munich-based sidekick of electro-legend Giorgio Moroder, its disco stylings were still faintly in vogue. But Elton played no instruments and wrote none of the songs, most of which were provided by Bellotte, and it opened with an eight-minute version of Chuck Berry's "Johnny B. Goode." Promotion was negligible, and Elton was happy to sweep it under the carpet as swiftly as possible, even if the title track, with backing vocals by Michael McDonald, was a minor US hit.

In reality Elton was a victim of poor health. He'd fallen ill at home in late '78. That familiar showbiz euphemism "exhaustion" was blamed. He was taken into a Harley Street coronary unit having collapsed, which suggests something more serious than exhaustion was afoot. This didn't stop him undertaking those Russian dates, and keeping it intimate with just Cooper as a sidekick meant less rigmarole than the glitz of the previous tours. That suited him now, and he seemed to draw most pleasure from his Watford FC associations, hosting garden parties for the team and staff at his Woodside manor, with its indoor pool, cinema, and disco.

Possibly he felt disconcerted by the slide in his musical fortunes. Dates in New York failed to sell out—an unthinkable occurrence just a couple of years earlier. A reviewer in L.A. wrote of him as "curiously dated" and pinned him as being "from another era." The seventies were over. Was one of its biggest stars, Elton John, being dismissed alongside that decade? Clearly, he'd have to find ways to readjust and reboot if he wanted to enjoy the eighties and onward. A true survivor, he did.

Elton and percussionist Ray Cooper outside the Summer Palace in St. Petersburg during a tour of the former Soviet Union, May 1979. John's concerts were the first by a Western rock star in the Eastern Bloc. Footage from the tour was made into the film *To Russia . . . With Elton.*

7

STILL STANDING

"I had everything but I had nothing. I needed the challenge of changing my life, making it more fulfilling and sharing. I could see myself ending up as an eccentric, living alone and being incredibly fussy, rather like Quentin Crisp. Except that I dust and he doesn't. I didn't want that."

ELTON JOHN

It'd be a more seamless Hollywood narrative if the eighties began with Elton blasting his way out of the doldrums instantaneously with a defiant roar of "I'm Still Standing." In fact, the rebound didn't fully take place until three years into the decade, after a few false restarts and moderate, less-than-triumphant albums. Around this time came the memorable tale that after a few nights of insomnia, Elton irately phoned one of his staff (or a hotel concierge) in the middle of a night of inclement weather and ordered them to make London less windy.

For someone whose career was by his high standards going through a dip, September 1980 was a happy reminder of just how big he remained. His free concert in Central Park on the thirteenth, in honor of John Lennon and sponsored by Calvin Klein, drew reportedly close to 400,000 spectators. If Elton was moved, his Donald Duck costume soon leavened the tone, and when he found onstage that it wasn't the most practical for sitting at a piano stool, he threw in a few giggles and quacking noises, rendering the likes of "Your Song" somewhat less romantic. His mood was lifting. Admit it, you didn't get quacking noises with Leonard Cohen.

His profile had been slightly rehabilitated by May 1980's album *21 at 33* (his twenty-first album, including lives and compilations, aged thirty-three). While not a classic, Bernie was back with (some) lyrics, while Gary Osborne provided others. Rocket signee Judie Tzuke, who'd given the label a hit with "Stay with Me till Dawn," co-wrote the final track, "Give Me the Love"; Tom Robinson another. It felt as if Elton was tentatively allowing his best collaborators back in. The underappreciated Clive Franks produced again, Dee Murray and Nigel Olsson returned for cameos, James Newton Howard was back, and of course Bernie's partial involvement improved the mood lighting. Top American names like Don Henley and Glenn Frey guested. Another guest was one Peter Noone. The album landed just outside the Top 10 in both the US and UK, while "Little Jeannie" gave Elton his first American top-three single in four years. Partly recorded during the same sessions, the May 1981 album *The Fox* consolidated this steady holding pattern musically, though it sold poorly. This despite signing to

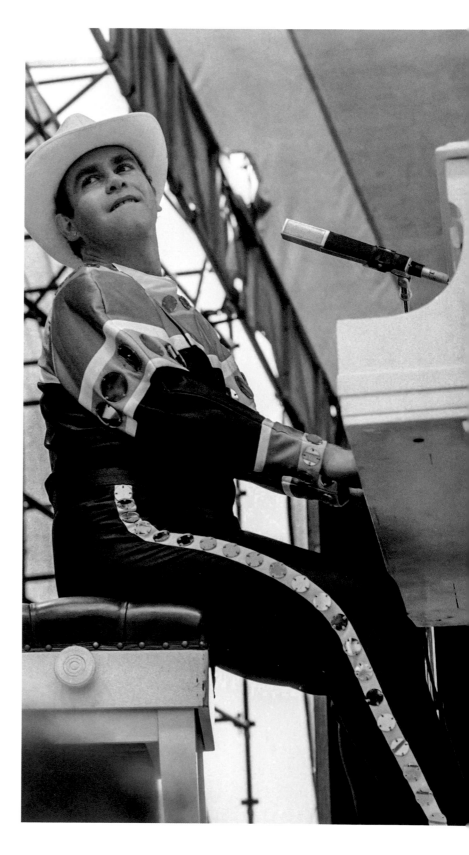

PREVIOUS PAGE: Shepperton Studios near London, filming a video for his album *The Fox*, June 1981.
RIGHT: Elton John gazes out at the sea of fans who turned out at New York's Central Park to see him perform in a free concert, September 13, 1980.

ELTON JOHN

2 1 A T 3 3

21 AT 33

TRACK LIST

SIDE ONE
Chasing the Crown
Little Jeannie
Sartorial Eloquence
Two Rooms at the End of the World

SIDE TWO
White Lady White Powder
Dear God
Never Gonna Fall in Love Again
Take Me Back
Give Me the Love

Recorded at Super Bear Studios, Nice, France; Rumbo Recorders and Sunset Sound, Los Angeles, USA
Produced by Elton John & Clive Franks
Released May 13, 1980
Label The Rocket Record Company, HISPD 126
Highest chart position on release UK 12, US 13, CAN 10, AUS 7, FRA 3, ITA 25, JPN 56, GER 21, NOR 6

KEY PERSONNEL
Elton John: lead and backing vocals, overdubbed piano, acoustic piano (1, 3, 5, 6, 8), Yamaha electric piano (4), Wurlitzer electric piano (8)
James Newton Howard: Fender Rhodes (2, 6, 7), Yamaha CS–80 (2), electronic keyboards (3, 7), acoustic piano (9)
Steve Lukather: electric guitar (1, 3, 4, 6, 7, 9)
Reggie McBride: bass guitar (1–4, 6–9)
Richie Zito: acoustic guitar (2, 7), electric guitar (5, 8)

COVER ART
George Osaki: art direction
Norman Moore: design and concept
Jim Shea: photography

NOTES
The title comes from the fact that this was John's 21st album in total at the age of 33.

Geffen in the States and bringing in producer Chris Thomas for the first time. An inauspicious start, perhaps, but Thomas, legendary for his work with everyone from the Beatles to Pink Floyd to Roxy Music to the Pretenders, was soon Elton's primary producer for a fruitful period. *The Fox* again shared out wordsmith tasks between Taupin and Osborne, as if Elton was playing the field. Taupin's titles, such as "Fascist Faces" and "Just Like Belgium," didn't lend themselves to potential pop hits, while another collaboration with Tom "Glad to Be Gay" Robinson spoke multitudes about a gay romance under the deceptively plain title of "Elton's Song." "Elton's gay video shocker," gasped the tabloids of its promo.

BELOW: Shepperton Studios near London, filming a video for his album *The Fox*, June 1981.
RIGHT: Sitting colorfully, poolside, 1981.

THE FOX

TRACK LIST

SIDE ONE
Breaking Down Barriers
Heart in the Right Place
Just Like Belgium
Nobody Wins
Fascist Faces

SIDE TWO
Carla Etude / Fanfare / Chloe
Heels of the Wind
Elton's Song
The Fox

Recorded at Super Bear Studios, Nice, France; Sunset Sound Recorders, the Village Recorder and Devlon Studios, Los Angeles, USA; Abbey Road Studios, London, England
Produced by Elton John, Chris Thomas & Clive Franks
Released May 20, 1981
Label The Rocket Record Company, TRAIN 16
Highest chart position on release UK 12, US 21, CAN 43, AUS 2, FRA 5, GER 34, NOR 5

KEY PERSONNEL
Elton John: lead vocals, backing vocals (1, 2, 4, 5, 9), piano (1–3, 5, 6, 8–11), vocal solo on "Breaking Down Barriers"
Dee Murray: bass guitar (1, 3, 5, 9, 11), backing vocals on "Chloe"
James Newton Howard: synthesizer (1–4, 7, 9, 10), vocoder (2), programming (4, 10), Fender Rhodes (8), Hammond organ (11)
Nigel Olsson: drums (1, 3, 5, 9, 11)
Richie Zito: guitar (1, 3, 5, 9, 11)

COVER ART
Richard Seireeni: art direction
Eric Blum: photography
Terry O'Neill: Elton John photograph

JUMP UP!

TRACK LIST

SIDE ONE
Dear John
Spiteful Child
Ball & Chain
Legal Boys
I Am Your Robot
Blue Eyes

SIDE TWO
Empty Garden
Princess
Where Have All the Good Times Gone?
All Quiet on the Western Front

Recorded at AIR Studios, Montserrat and Pathé-Marconi Studios, Paris, France
Produced by Chris Thomas
Released April 9, 1982
Label The Rocket Record Company, HISPD 127
Highest chart position on release UK 13, US 17, CAN 19, AUS 3, FRA 12, GER 47, NOR 3

KEY PERSONNEL
Elton John: lead vocals, backing vocals, piano, harpsichord on "Empty Garden"
Pete Townshend: acoustic guitar on "Ball and Chain"
James Newton Howard: synthesizers, Fender Rhodes, strings and brass arrangement
Dee Murray: bass guitar, backing vocals
Jeff Porcaro: drums, percussion
Richie Zito: guitar

COVER ART
David Costa: art direction
David Nutter: photography

> ## One of our worst albums . . . but it had 'Empty Garden' on it, so it's worth it for that one song.

BERNIE TAUPIN

Released in April '82, *Jump Up!* was another water-treader, even if Chris Thomas was now ensconced as producer. Again, it just tickled the edges of the Top 10 in Britain and the US, with the affecting "Blue Eyes" the only hit single and a reminder of how emotionally resonant Elton's melodies could be when he was at his best. Taupin and Osborne's monopoly on lyrics was this time broken by acclaimed lyricist Tim Rice, who co-wrote "Legal Boys" and would later become a close collaborator. Pete Townshend guested on "Ball and Chain." Taupin's "Empty Garden (Hey Hey Johnny)" was a tribute to the late John Lennon, who'd been killed a year and a half before, and referenced his and Elton's Madison Square Garden moments. Taupin wrote the lyrics the day after Lennon died. He later defended this song while trashing the album. On a 2010 Sirius radio special, he dismissed *Jump Up!* as "one of our worst albums . . . but it had 'Empty Garden' on it, so it's worth it for that one song." *Creem* magazine referred to Elton as "Ol' Four Eyes" but suggested it was the best pop album he'd made. A Hammersmith Odeon concert saw Elton dressed in a by-all-accounts outrageous mock-military costume, complete with breeches and hat, and caused a furor when Elton went through his customary action of kicking his piano stool away only for it to hit a young woman in the front row, who was slightly injured. Elton afterwards met and apologized to her, showering her with gifts.

Luckily for Bernie, Elton, and listeners alike, the next album was the true comeback kid. It reunited the band—Johnstone, Murray, Olsson, Cooper—and gave Elton his first UK Top 10 album for five years. More than that, it stuck around on the UK and US charts for over a year. *Too Low for Zero* was a renaissance both artistically and commercially. In John Tobler's liner notes for the 1998 reissue, Bernie said it was "another turning point, because it came on the heels of Elton and I writing sporadically

In militray uniform, Hammersmith Odeon, London, December 1982.

together over the two previous years. We'd started working together again, but this was our first total commitment, and it worked." Elton was keen to emphasize therein that had never been a quarrel, or at least not to the extent the press had insinuated. "Let's clear up this misconception. I was living in England, Bernie was living in the US, but we never at any time in our lives fell out with each other or had arguments. It was never, ever a split. It was just a healthy time apart. If we hadn't had that break, we might never have survived."

Indeed, Elton had survived the first real winter of his career. The morose opening track, "Cold as Christmas" gave way to the buoyant anthem that was "I'm Still Standing." It had been no picnic finding the route to this resurgence. "Drugs, sex and doomed liaisons were my form of destruction," he later confessed. There had been a number of unsatisfactory short-term romances. One was Vance, the subject of "Blue Eyes," who later tragically died of AIDS. Another was Gary Clarke, who kissed and told in a book. The cocaine was hindering Elton's wisdom when it came to selectivity. Watford manager Graham Taylor was a big help, doing all he could to get his unlikely close friend off the booze and drugs. "He brought me to my senses," said the singer. And according to an interview Elton gave with *Rolling Stone* in 2002, former Beatle George Harrison also gave him a few good sharp lectures. He witnessed Elton trying to persuade Bob Dylan to dress up in gaudy Versace in L.A. one night and said, "Listen, for God's sake go easy on the marching powder—it's not going to do you any good." Gary Osborne has also spoken of distressing scenes. As the singles from the likes of *21 at 33* and *The Fox* failed to set the world alight, the star was sometimes reclusive, losing himself in late-night poker games with Osborne.

At the same time, Elton kept it together enough to play at royal invitation, the Windsors being practically his neighbors. Prince Andrew's twenty-first birthday celebration in June 1981 at Windsor Castle was an early entry into his soon-to-be ongoing rapport with the royals. Newspapers reported—perhaps with a degree of speculation—that he'd danced the night away with the Queen and Princess Anne.

Yet now "I'm Still Standing," a self-fulfilling prophecy, was seeing Elton rebranded and reassessed. It was the video age, and Russell Mulcahy's Cannes-shot video for the song, casting Elton as a kind of lovable Charlie Chaplin amid girls in swimsuits, served its purpose. It might have been better if Elton hadn't gone off

TOP: Partying hard with Rod and Alana Stewart at the Elysées Matignon, Paris, 1981.
BOTTOM: With the original members of his band, 1982. L–R: Davey Johnston, guitar; Elton John; Nigel Olsson, drums; and Dave Murray, bass.

ELTON JOHN

TOO LOW FOR ZERO

TOO LOW FOR ZERO

TRACK LIST

SIDE ONE
Cold as Christmas (In the Middle of the Year)
I'm Still Standing
Too Low for Zero
Religion
I Guess That's Why They Call It the Blues

SIDE TWO
Crystal
Kiss the Bride
Whipping Boy
Saint
One More Arrow

Recorded at AIR Studios, Montserrat and Sunset Sound Recorders, Hollywood, USA
Produced by Chris Thomas
Released May 30, 1983
Label The Rocket Record Company, HISPD 24
Highest chart position on release UK 7, US 25, CAN 17, AUS 2, FRA 11, JPN 71, SPA 7, GER 5, NOR 6

KEY PERSONNEL
Elton John: piano (1–5, 8, 10), Fender Rhodes (1), synthesizer (1–7, 9) clavinet (9), lead and backing vocals
Davey Johnstone: acoustic guitar (1, 4, 5, 6, 9), electric guitar (2–10) backing vocals
Dee Murray: bass guitar, backing vocals
Nigel Olsson: drums, tambourine on "Whipping Boy", backing vocals
Kiki Dee: backing vocals on "Cold as Christmas (In the Middle of the Year)"
Stevie Wonder: harmonica on "I Guess That's Why They Call It the Blues"

COVER ART
Rod Dyer: art direction
Clive Piercy: design

LEFT: Still standing and smiling in China, 1983.
RIGHT: In concert at the Irvine Meadows, California, September 1984.

after the first day and got so drunk with Duran Duran front man Simon Le Bon that he reportedly came back bent on performing striptease in front of the camera, rolling around naked on the floor, only to wake up the next day wondering why he had so many bumps and bruises. Thankfully for all, footage has never emerged. Elton was never keen on making videos, wanting to do the bare minimum, but now began reluctantly to grasp their importance at this time. It worked, and the innate song-craft of *Too Low for Zero* was sold with the aid of high concept.

"I'm Still Standing," obvious choice as it would seem, wasn't in fact the first hit in the UK. "I Guess That's Why They Call It the Blues," its lilting melody co-written by Davey Johnstone, had that honor, its memorable refrains decorated by a cute Stevie Wonder harmonica solo. "I'm Still Standing" was, however, the first US release, and Elton has recalled it being "a great song to sing. At that point I was struggling with my American record company [Geffen], and it was kind of defiant." Oddly, it didn't make the US Top 10, though both singles went top five in the UK, his best phase in years. "Kiss the Bride" followed, its riff

faintly echoing "The Bitch Is Back," while "Cold as Christmas" (with old pal Kiki Dee guesting) was released for Xmas '83. Among the album's other highlights were the breakneck vocal delivery of "Crystal" and the more pensive "One More Arrow."

Gary Osborne felt that, while he understood the desire to get the old team back together, his part in keeping Elton afloat and active during the semi-wilderness years was being underappreciated by John Reid. "By then Elton had started touring again, so the money was coming back in, and by 1983 I had outgrown my usefulness." Taupin was pleased with his renewed "closeness and understanding" with Elton; it felt more like the creativity of their productive beginnings. He had remarried, to Toni Lynn Russo, and so found fresh areas of inspiration. Osborne remains philosophical, telling Elton biographer David Buckley: "I am standing in a house bought by 'Blue Eyes' and looking at the sea. I'm a lucky fucker."

Punk had popped its bubble, and in the year of Michael Jackson's *Thriller*, stars like Bowie, Rod Stewart, and Elton were reclaiming their positions atop the big leagues. Chris Thomas

LEFT: Performing in drag, Paris, May 1984.
RIGHT: In a Mother Goose costume at the London Palladium, December 1984.

BREAKING HEARTS

TRACK LIST

SIDE ONE
Restless
Slow Down Georgie (She's Poison)
Who Wears These Shoes?
Breaking Hearts (Ain't What It Used to Be)
Li'l 'Frigerator

SIDE TWO
Passengers
In Neon
Burning Buildings
Did He Shoot Her?
Sad Songs (Say So Much)

Recorded at AIR Studios, Montserrat
Produced by Chris Thomas
Released June 18, 1984
Label The Rocket Record Company, HISPD 25
Highest chart position on release UK 2, US 20, CAN 10,
AUS 1, JPN 54, SPA 5, GER 5, NOR 7

KEY PERSONNEL
Elton John: piano (3, 4, 5, 7, 8, 9, 10), synthesizer (1, 2, 3, 5, 6, 7, 9, 10), Hammond organ (5), harmonium (6), Fender Rhodes (7), harpsichord (7), clavinet (10), lead and backing vocals
Davey Johnstone: acoustic guitar (2, 6, 7, 8, 10), electric guitar (1–3, 5, 7, 8, 9), sitar (9), backing vocals (1–4, 6–10)
Dee Murray: bass guitar (1–3, 5–10), backing vocals (1–4, 6–10)
Nigel Olsson: drums (1–3, 5–10), backing vocals (1–4, 6–10)
Andrew Thompson: saxophone (5)

COVER ART
David Costa: art direction and design
Richard Young: photography
Patrick Jones: band photography

had now proven his worth, and with Elton's appetite re-whetted, the team reconvened at AIR Studios in Montserrat to start work on a follow-up. It would be the last to feature all the key members of the classic Elton John band: bassist Dee Murray passed away in 1992 and Olsson didn't play drums on an Elton album again until 2001. It was also the last on which Elton played all keyboards himself. Thomas, too, was on limited time, with Gus Dudgeon back in the producer's chair next time round. But this was all in the future, as the team settled in to a relaxed set of sessions through late '83 and early '84. Ultimately, *Breaking Hearts* turned out to be a mild disappointment, with "Sad Songs (Say So Much)" and "Passengers" its best outings, those two hit singles taking the album to No. 2 in the UK (and No. 20 in the US). Most people's takeaway from the video for the former was that Elton wasn't, in some scenes, wearing his glasses. "Passengers" was largely based on a South African folk tune, with Phineas Mkhize sharing writing credits. However, its nods to anti-racism and anti-apartheid were undermined by the star playing four big shows with Rod Stewart at the Sun City two hours northwest of Johannesburg, ignoring the UN's cultural boycott of South Africa.

Breaking Hearts may be best immortalized as the background music to a curious episode in Elton's personal life. Its German recording engineer, Renate Blauel, became friendly with the singer in Montserrat. In her late twenties, she'd worked briefly on an Elton session in London before, and he now insisted she become part of the team. She was popular, efficient, friendly. All involved were however surprised when Elton excitedly rang around announcing that he and Renate were getting married. "Elton John to Wed!" screamed the headlines, which bemused most of his friends and family, given his not-exactly-secret sexuality. Yet those close to the pair have said they seemed genuinely to have fallen in love with each other. Elton very much wanted children. On Valentine's Day 1984, they did indeed marry, at St. Mark's Church in Sydney, with Elton's former beau John Reid as best man. A costly reception ensued for the touring crew, who mixed glee and bewilderment. He thanked Chris Thomas for his encouragement and help, adding that he'd chosen Australia to avoid (as much as possible) the British press. Some posited the slightly cynical theory that he was trying to win back areas of America who didn't look kindly on homosexuality or bisexuality. But those in close proximity emphasized that he and Renate had a real friendship. Friendship is perhaps the key word here, despite the optimistic beginnings. Journalist Nina Myskow interviewed for Philip Norman's 2002 biography, *Sir Elton*, revealed that Elton told her that, "when he saw Renate coming down the aisle towards him, he thought she was the most beautiful thing he'd ever seen in his life. And there were tears in his eyes when he said it." She's added that, "she

Elton's and Renate Blauel's wedding, St. Mark's Church, Sydney, February 14, 1984.

was a really intelligent, lively girl" and "modest and unassertive. She knew just the way to get along with Elton. When they were together, they were good together." She insisted that there was a physical side to the relationship, and at first he lavished gifts and attention on her as she moved in to his Windsor mansion.

He told the *Daily Express*'s David Wigg: "I had everything but I had nothing. I needed the challenge of changing my life, making it more fulfilling and sharing. I could see myself ending up as an eccentric, living alone and being incredibly fussy, rather like Quentin Crisp. Except that I dust and he doesn't. I didn't want that." Marriage, he said, was "fabulous. I'm so happy, and very much in love. I'm calmer, less argumentative now, and more reasonable. I don't get my own way anymore, but it's so nice to

I'm so happy, and very much in love. I'm calmer, less argumentative now, and more reasonable.

ELTON JOHN

Elton and new wife Renate share a kiss, 1984.

come home and actually share things." Compromise may have been eased by the fact that Renate had her own suite of rooms. "There's a woman's touch, and I like that." He talked often about his desire to have children. Having not enjoyed being an only child, he emphasized the plural. He was, however, soon away on tours again, which suggested that it was easier to keep the idealized illusion afloat if they weren't actually hemmed in living together every day.

Years on, however, Elton looked back at the marriage, which lasted four years before divorce, and posted on social media, "I got married because I didn't confront the real problem in my life—that I was a drug addict. I thought getting married would change all the unhappiness the drugs brought me. I got married to a wonderful woman who loved me very much. I loved her, but not in the physical sense. I thought that would change. I thought: now I'll become happy. But the problem was I still stuck cocaine up my nose and drank a bottle of Scotch a day.

Nothing changed." Thousands of people loved him when he was onstage, but offstage he felt little, or nothing.

He was cheered up by Watford FC's journey to the 1984 FA Cup Final. As underdogs, they lost to Everton, but what Elton labeled "the biggest day of my life" (just a few months after his wedding) moved him to tears of pride. And he was back at Wembley Stadium the following summer for an even bigger event. The Live Aid concert on July 13, 1985, was a massive fundraising phenomenon, initiated by Bob Geldof and Midge Ure and, together with concerts that day in Philadelphia and across the world, was watched by a TV audience of around forty percent of the global population. A-listers lined up to play, both for a fine cause and (cynics might say) for a vast captive crowd.

RIGHT: In concert, at New York's Madison Square Garden, October 1984.
BELOW: At Wembley Stadium after his club, Watford, was beaten in the FA Cup final, May 19, 1984.

Everyone remembers Wembley's legendary performances that day, with Queen and U2 among the most prominent. the Who, Bowie, and Paul McCartney also gave their best. Elton's twenty-five-minute set (technically second on the bill to McCartney, and one of the lengthier sets) was introduced by his buddy, comedian Billy Connolly, and also featured moments of magic, some planned, some—like a sudden burst of rain on what had been a very hot, sunny day—beyond his control. Sporting a stripy, shiny frock coat, he opened with "I'm Still Standing," "Bennie and the Jets," and "Rocket Man" before Kiki Dee joined him for "Don't Go Breaking My Heart." Then came George Michael's onstage arrival (and that of Wham's Andrew Ridgeley, less heralded) for "Don't Let the Sun Go Down on Me." Six years later, a live version from Michael's Wembley Arena show, with Elton in the guest role, became a Grammy-nominated No. 1 on both sides of the Atlantic.

Like most acts involved, Elton tried to capitalize on Live Aid's profile with a new album, and when Gus Dudgeon came back to the fold as producer, with songs written by John and Taupin and recorded at SOL Studio, things augured well. *Ice on Fire*, released in November, didn't melt fans' hearts however, proving a relative flop in America despite reaching the British top three. It did yield two hit singles, both of which featured new best pal George Michael. "Nikita" was a curious ballad describing a crush on an unattainable (for geopolitical reasons) East German border guard. Its video was directed by Ken Russell and included a fantasy scene where Elton and "Nikita" wore

ABOVE: Live Aid, Wembley Stadium, July 13, 1985. L–R: Bob Geldof, Adam Ant, Elton John, Gary Kemp, Tony Hadley, and Midge Ure.
RIGHT: George Michael and Elton, backstage after their performance together at Live Aid, Wembley.

ELTON JOHN
ICE ON FIRE

ICE ON FIRE

TRACK LIST

SIDE ONE
This Town
Cry to Heaven
Soul Glove
Nikita
Too Young

SIDE TWO
Wrap Her Up
Satellite
Tell Me What the Papers Say
Candy by the Pound
Shoot Down the Moon

Recorded at the SOL Studio, Cookham and CTS studios, Wembley, England
Produced by Gus Dudgeon
Released November 4, 1985
Label The Rocket Record Company, HISPD 26
Highest chart position on release UK 3, US 48, CAN 49, AUS 6, SPA 6, GER 5, NOR 2

KEY PERSONNEL
Elton John: lead vocals, acoustic piano (1–3, 5, 8, 10, 11), Yamaha GS1 piano (4, 5), synthesizer (4, 7, 9, 11), backing vocals (4)
Davey Johnstone: electric guitar (1, 3, 5, 6, 8, 9, 11), Spanish guitar (2), synth guitar (2, 7), backing vocals (3, 5, 6–9)
Deon Estus: bass guitar (3, 7, 11)
Mel Gaynor: drums (3, 7, 11)
Fred Mandel: synthesizers (1, 4, 5, 10, 11), keyboards (2, 3, 6–9), sequencer (6), electric guitar (7, 11), finger snaps (7), arrangements (10)

COVER ART
David Larkham: art direction and design
Terry O'Neill: photography

Watford football shirts. The tangent that Nikita is a male name in Russian fostered some gossip. Nik Kershaw joined George on backing vocals and played guitar. Follow-up "Wrap Her Up," a minor hit, was arguably more interesting, as it saw Elton listing a catalog of glamorous women, from Marlene Dietrich and Rita Hayworth through to Joan Collins and, dating it somewhat, Samantha Fox. George Michael told *Smash Hits* that his falsetto on it "sounded like I had my willy in a garrote." Perhaps *Ice on Fire* was a missed opportunity, with Dudgeon trying too hard to make it sound mid-eighties (all synth-drums and keyboards) instead of tapping into the old team's strengths.

Compared to October 1986's album *Leather Jackets*, though, it was a triumph. This, again produced by Dudgeon, with what should have been a dream team—plus cameos from Queen's Roger Taylor and John Deacon, a duet with Cliff Richard ("Slow Rivers"), a song co-written by Cher, and one featuring the writing return of Gary Osborne—was the first to fail to find a Top 40 single since *Tumbleweed Connection*. In 2006, Elton cited it as his least favorite of all, confessing to *Mojo* that "Gus did his best, but you can't work with a loony." In 1997, he'd told the

ABOVE: Andrew Ridgeley (center) and George Michael (right) of Wham! with Elton, backstage at their farewell concert, entitled *The Final*, Wembley Stadium, London June 28, 1986.
RIGHT: Elton and Millie Jackson performing in the video for "Act of War," 1985.

same magazine: "A total disaster. I was not a well budgie. I was married and it was just one bag of coke after another." So much for wedded bliss. Dudgeon told VH1 in 2000 that "there was a real chance he'd polish himself off. He'd go out and do some coke and it'd be all over his mouth, his nose would be running, and I'd go, 'Oh God, this is just awful.'" Unsurprisingly, it was the last Elton John studio album produced by Gus, and Chris Thomas bravely stepped forth again two years later for the next. By then, the man who'd sung for his supper all his life had undergone surgery on his vocal cords.

There had been brighter moments during this phase. A live orchestral version of "Candle in the Wind" had finally made it a major US hit, and Elton's participation in "That's What Friends Are For," the charity single for AIDS research released under the group name Dionne & Friends, was the Grammy-winning, US best-selling single of '86. Written by Burt Bacharach and Carole Bayer Sager, it had first been recorded by Rod Stewart in '82, but now gathered Dionne Warwick, Stevie Wonder, Gladys Knight, and Elton. It raised over $3 million for its cause. Not averse to pursuing fun, Elton had also worked with Millie Jackson and, perhaps more surprisingly, played piano on an album by Brit heavy metal chuggers Saxon. He also appeared on the BBC radio show *Desert Island Discs*, interviewed by Michael Parkinson and talking candidly of his life as he chose music by Edward Elgar, Thelonius Monk, and Nina Simone.

LEATHER JACKETS

TRACK LIST

SIDE ONE
Leather Jackets
Hoop of Fire
Don't Trust That Woman
Go It Alone
Gypsy Heart

SIDE TWO
Slow Rivers
Heartache All Over the World
Angeline
Memory of Love
Paris
I Fall Apart

Recorded at Wisseloord Studios, Hilversum, Netherlands; CTS Studios, Wembley and the SOL Studio, Cookham, England
Produced by Gus Dudgeon
Released October 15, 1986
Label The Rocket Record Company, EJLP 1
Highest chart position on release UK 24, US 91, CAN 38, AUS 4, NLD 34, GER 21, NOR 12

KEY PERSONNEL
Elton John: vocals, Yamaha GS1 (1, 8), piano (2, 4–6, 10), Roland JX-8P (2, 11), MIDI piano (3), Yamaha CP-80 (11)
Davey Johnstone: acoustic guitar (1–5, 7, 9), electric guitar (2–11), backing vocals (2, 4, 5, 7–10)
Fred Mandel: synthesizer, programming, sequencer (1, 4, 7), Yamaha DX7 (2, 6, 9), Korg DW-8000 (3, 10), Roland JX-8P (4, 11), Roland Jupiter 8 (5, 6, 10, 11), Roland P60 (7, 9), Prophet 2000 (7), Yamaha TX816 Fender Rhodes (10), piano (11)
Charlie Morgan: drums (2, 4, 6, 7, 9–11), percussion (4)
David Paton: bass guitar (2, 3, 5, 9–11)

COVER ART
David Costa: art direction and design
Gered Mankowitz: photography

He needed the release. Marriage to Renate, clearly, had not been the magic cure-all he'd fantasized about, and the drug abuse was out of control. There was more bad news breaking, but in retrospect it seems the next bout with misery pressed him into kicking some of those nasty habits.

The press were cruelly painting Elton and Renate's marriage as "shaky" on an almost daily basis, constantly referencing his "gay past." She was rarely seen in public with him, only occasionally accompanying him to awards ceremonies. She was with him when he began his latest four-night run at Madison Square Garden, and it was during these shows that his voice started faltering and breaking up. The last night was especially awkward. Putting on a brave face, he returned to London and did Terry Wogan's TV show wearing a yellow fright wig and huge silver wings. "I'm forty next year," he reasoned. "People expect me to make a fool of myself. And I always do." Yet

on a subsequent Australian tour, the voice packed in again. Concerts were cancelled. He couldn't even speak. Eventually, he was persuaded to consult serious specialists. Nodules were discovered around his vocal cords. He told friends he was frightened, even if he maintained his bravado in public. He rang his mother. In January 1987, he was operated on in Sydney, and the nodules, it transpired, were benign. He was told, to his immense relief, that he'd make a complete recovery and, if he convalesced sensibly, would sing freely again. Happy news, even if the tabloids were more preoccupied with Renate's absence from his bedside.

The sleazy hysteria reached a manic peak when the *Sun* came out with a front-page story claiming "Elton in Vice Boys Scandal." Yet the paper misstepped by muddling up dates. On one on which it accused Elton of scandalous behavior in England, he'd been on a flight from New York. This opened the paper up to a massive lawsuit. There were those who advised Elton against it, such as Mick Jagger, who thought the *Sun* would only double down. The *Sun* did just that with more inflammatory headlines a few days later, but the *Daily Mirror* leapt to Elton's defense, letting readers know the star had been five thousand miles away from the "homosexual orgy" the *Sun* had written about. And in 1988, Elton won the libel case. "I've won," he told Nina Myskow, as reported in Philip Norman's book *Sir Elton*, "The *Sun* are going to pay me a million pounds." The paper also ran a front page headline: "SORRY, ELTON".

The same year, as if in defiance, Elton acquired his very own coat of arms. The crest showed piano keys, records, and the colors of Watford FC. The motto read in Spanish: "*el tono es bueso*"—which translates as "the tone is good" while punning on his name. Later, the steel helmet and open visor came to indicate his knighthood.

> "I'm forty next year. People expect me to make a fool of myself. And I always do.

ELTON JOHN

LEFT: Elton and Renate at the Ivor Novello Awards ceremony, April 1986.
BELOW: Under fire in the press, Elton fights back, London 1988.

His fortieth birthday party at John Reid's home, Lockwell House in Hertfordshire, on March 26th, 1987, was a flush celebration. From George and Ringo to Eric Clapton, Phil Collins, and Bob Geldof, from Richard Branson and Ken Russell to the Watford football team, the guest list was stellar. He apologized for Renate's absence. Squeezed by the press, Reid's office announced the next day that Elton and Renate had decided to "continue living apart." The papers soon discovered that she'd moved to an expensive flat (paid for by Elton) in Kensington. It wasn't over yet: there remained genuine affection between the couple. But by November '88 it was official: an amicable divorce settlement was reached, and both retained some dignity, speaking only highly of each other.

By now, Elton had officially come out. The album *Reg Strikes Back,* released in 1988, was his way of venting against the press harassment, and while its Top 20 placings in the UK and US were mediocre, it confirmed that his voice was still functioning (though in a significantly lower register from here on because of the surgery), and wouldn't be silenced. "Mona Lisas and Mad Hatters, Part Two" was an intriguing sequel to its *Honky Château* predecessor, while "I Don't Wanna Go On with You Like That" was an American No. 2. This was Dee Murray's last Elton album before his death in 1992.

CLOCKWISE FROM LEFT: Looking fabulous in Sydney, 1987; Bernie Taupin, Cher, Whoopi Goldberg, and Elton John at the MTV Music Video Awards, 1987; Onstage at a charity gala in aid of the Prince's Trust, Wembley Stadium, London, June 1987; Elton's 40th birthday, the morning after, Lockwell House, March 27, 1987.

REG STRIKES BACK

TRACK LIST

SIDE ONE
Town of Plenty
A Word in Spanish
Mona Lisas and Mad Hatters, Part Two
I Don't Wanna Go On with You Like That
Japanese Hands

SIDE TWO
Goodbye Marlon Brando
The Camera Never Lies
Heavy Traffic
Poor Cow
Since God Invented Girls

Recorded at AIR Studios and Westside Studios, London, England; Circle Seven Recording and the Record Plant, Los Angeles, USA
Produced by Chris Thomas
Released June 24, 1988
Label The Rocket Record Company, EJLP 3
Highest chart position on release UK 18, US 16, CAN 6, AUS 12, FRA 30, ITA 3, GER 18, NOR 8

KEY PERSONNEL

Elton John: keyboards, backing vocals, lead and harmony vocals
Fred Mandel: synthesizer
Davey Johnstone: guitar, backing vocals
Pete Townshend: acoustic guitar on "Town of Plenty"
David Paton: bass guitar
Charlie Morgan: drums

COVER ART

David Costa: art direction and design
Gered Mankowitz: photography

Elton John at
the auction of
his memorabilia
and artifacts at
Sotheby's, London,
1988.

SLEEPING WITH THE PAST

TRACK LIST

SIDE ONE
Durban Deep
Healing Hands
Whispers
Club at the End of the Street
Sleeping with the Past

SIDE TWO
Stone's Throw from Hurtin'
Sacrifice
I Never Knew Her Name
Amazes Me
Blue Avenue

Recorded at Puk Recording Studios, Randers, Denmark
Produced by Chris Thomas
Released March 29, 1989
Label The Rocket Record Company, EJLP 4
Highest chart position on release UK 1, US 23, CAN 23, AUS 2, FRA 2, ITA 6, GER 9, NOR 4, SPA 3

KEY PERSONNEL
Elton John: keyboards, lead and harmony vocals, backing vocals (1)
Guy Babylon: keyboards
Davey Johnstone: guitar, backing vocals (tracks 1, 2, 4, 5, 6, 8, 9, 10)
Fred Mandel: keyboards (1, 2, 3, 5, 7, 9, 10), guitar (1, 4, 8), organ (4), guitar solo (6)
Romeo Williams: bass guitar
Jonathan Moffett: drums

COVER ART
Wherefor Art?: art direction and design
Herb Ritts: photography

BELOW: The angelic, psychedelic mohawk look, London 1988.
BELOW RIGHT: Performing in New York, 1988.

Elton's 1989 album *Sleeping with the Past* built on this show of resilience and resistance. To his delight, "Sacrifice" gave him his first UK No. 1 single, and the album, influenced by soul and R&B, shrugged off lukewarm reviews to match that chart placing. Going platinum, it was the first wholly John-Taupin album (with no other writers involved) since *Captain Fantastic.* "Sacrifice" is an odd song to have rescued a career; on first listen it's a nothing-special sleepy ballad, a production of its time. Yet its subtle Aretha-meets-Percy-Sledge heritage gives it some emotional pull, which obviously resonated with a public willing

Elton to be a winner given his brave stance against the press. Some noted an undertow of "Your Song." Bernie Taupin has said it's one of the best songs the pair ever wrote.

It was in every sense a slow burner and didn't take off until 1990. After a sometimes ebullient but often bruising eighties, Elton wasn't merely still standing. That true survivor had earned the renewed affection of the public, beaten the bully boys of Fleet Street, and was enjoying his very first solo No. 1 single in his homeland as a new decade began. He was ready to pick up the pieces of his life. It would be kinder to him.

In Paris during
his Reg Strikes
Back tour,
March 1989.

Elton John
attends the
Victoires de
la Musique
ceremony in
Paris, February
1990.

8

ENGLAND'S ROSE

"They don't come much bigger than this. I've had a long career and worked hard. But I think the turning point came in 1990 when I got sober, and decided to do some charity work, particularly for the AIDS problem. A knighthood is the icing on the cake."

ELTON JOHN

With the soft power of "Sacrifice" staying at No. 1 for six weeks, Elton was very much, as they say, back, with his productivity again almost matching his celebrity. His guest appearance on George Michael's live cover of "Don't Let the Sun Go Down on Me" provided another No. 1 a year later (both in the US and the UK), and he won Best British Male Solo Artist at the Brit Awards. This was the decade he'd throw himself into important charity work and pick up an Oscar, a Hall of Fame recognition, a knighthood, best-selling records, and a new life partner, but there would be some challenges as the decade wore on.

Managed again for a time by John Reid, in June 1992, he released *The One*, after sessions in Paris's Studio Guillame Tell, with Chris Thomas producing. The cover artwork was by Gianni Versace and the album was dedicated to Vance Buck, the American nightclub and fashion entrepreneur who'd had a long relationship with the singer, inspiring "Blue Eyes." The pair had been introduced by Andy Warhol in New York in the late seventies. Found to be HIV positive in '86, Buck was ailing now, and he died a month after *The One* paid tribute to him. Impressions of the album were shaded by the odd decision to place focus on the duet with Eric Clapton, "Runaway Train," and the accompanying dates featuring Elton as a part-time member of Clapton's live band. Otherwise, the title track, "The Last Song," and "Simple Life" were solid hits. It was, however, a John-Taupin album, with Davey Johnstone, Nigel Olsson, and Kiki Dee guesting, not to mention Pink Floyd's David Gilmour on "Understanding Women."

At least, as he's confessed, a now abstinent (from drink and drugs) Elton remembered recording this one. He'd undertaken a serious rehab course after his addictions had bitten back again, and he'd in parallel suffered from bulimia. This latter problem was something over which he'd come to bond with Princess Diana, offering her advice from experience. And his new image as clean-living Elton may have convinced Warner/Chappell Music, in November '92, to give Bernie Taupin and him the biggest advance in the history of music publishing at that time. The pair signed their publishing deal for a reported $40 million across twelve years. The *Los Angeles Times* described

it as "more than twice the previous highest advance," which had reportedly been paid to Prince earlier the same year. The company thus took the rights to all the pair's material since 1974, plus the songs from forthcoming albums. In a low-key comment, for him, Elton simply and diplomatically remarked, "I've always had a great relationship with Warner/Chappell and I'm very pleased with the way this deal turned out." Fans reflected approvingly on the fact that it bound him to write with Bernie for some time ahead.

His profile was not ebbing. That spring he'd appeared at the Freddie Mercury tribute concert at Wembley Stadium, singing Queen's "The Show Must Go On" with the band's surviving members and taking part in an all-star rendition of "Bohemian Rhapsody." Mercury had died from AIDS-related complications in the fall of 1991. David Bowie, George Michael,

PREVIOUS PAGE: Onstage at Madison Square Garden, October 1998.
RIGHT: Poster for the Elton John and Eric Clapton concert at Wembley Stadium, June 1992.

THE ONE

TRACK LIST

Simple Life
The One
Sweat It Out
Runaway Train
Whitewash County
The North
When a Woman Doesn't Want You
Emily
On Dark Street
Understanding Women
The Last Song

Recorded at Studio Guillame Tell, Paris, France
Produced by Chris Thomas
Released June 22, 1992
Label The Rocket Record Company, 512 360-2
Highest chart position on release UK 2, US 8, CAN 7, AUS 2, FRA 1, ITA 1, GER 1, NOR 2, SPA 4, JPN 35

KEY PERSONNEL

Elton John: keyboards, vocals
Davey Johnstone: guitar (2–5, 7–9), backing vocals (7, 9)
Olle Romo: drums, percussion, programming (1–10)
Pino Palladino: bass guitar (1–8, 10)
Mark Taylor: keyboards (1–3, 6, 7)
Guy Babylon: keyboards, programming (2–5, 7–11)
Adam Seymour: guitar (1, 2, 6, 7)

COVER ART

Gianni Versace: art direction and design
Patrick Dermarchelier: photography

Roger Daltrey, Robert Plant, U2, Axl Rose and Slash of Guns N' Roses, and Annie Lennox were among those also paying their respects in front of a 71,000 crowd and live TV audiences across seventy-six countries. Profits went to AIDS charity the Mercury Phoenix Trust.

The Guns N' Roses connection was a strange but briefly stable one: the odd couple of Elton and Axl bonded, and at the MTV Video Music Awards in '92 the Brit joined the fast-rising American rockers for a version of their "November Rain." Indeed, he was nurturing new networks everywhere, forming friendships with stars old and new. Confirming this was *Duets*, the 1993 album on which he paired up on classic soul and pop songs with everybody from the hero of his youth Little Richard to then-popular hip-hop subverters P.M. Dawn. In between, indicating Elton's enduring starry pulling power, there were duets with greats like Leonard Cohen, Gladys Knight, Tammy Wynette, and that chart-topping George Michael collaboration. Also linking up, in a borderline surreal set of industry-straddling names, were Don Henley, Nik Kershaw,

Paul Young, k.d. lang, Marcella Detroit, Bonnie Raitt, Chris Rea, Kiki Dee (with whom he sang Cole Porter's "True Love," which gave them a top-three hit), and RuPaul (who put a new spin on Kiki's role in "Don't Go Breaking My Heart"). As if that wasn't enough, producers of individual tracks included Giorgio Moroder, Stevie Wonder, Narada Michael Walden, and Don Was. And whereas Frank Sinatra would put together such an album without ever meeting most of his singing partners, Elton did so by being in the studio with them for each track. Moments where his new best friends click musically with his now AOR style are few, but the spirit was willing. If he'd thrown everything (from every genre) at the wall here, it only

FAR LEFT: Elton and Axl Rose performing live onstage at the Freddie Mercury Tribute Concert, April 20, 1992.
ABOVE LEFT: Elton and Brian May at the funeral of Freddie Mercury, November 1991.
ABOVE RIGHT: Elton's floral tribute to Freddie: "Thankyou for being my friend, I will love you always".

ELTON JOHN

DUETS

DUETS

TRACK LIST

Teardrops (with k.d. lang)
When I Think About Love (I Think About You) (with P.M. Dawn)
The Power (with Little Richard)
Shakey Ground (with Don Henley)
True Love (with Kiki Dee)
If You Were Me (with Chris Rea)
A Woman's Needs (with Tammy Wynette)
Old Friend (with Nik Kershaw)
Go On And On (with Gladys Knight)
Don't Go Breaking My Heart (with Ru Paul)
Ain't Nothing Like the Real Thing (with Marcella Detroit)
I'm Your Puppet (with Paul Young)
Love Letters (with Bonnie Raitt)
Born to Lose (with Leonard Cohen)
Don't Let the Sun Go Down on Me (with George Michael)
Duets for One

Recorded at Ocean Way Recording, Conway Recording Studios & Capitol Studios, Hollywood; A&M Studios & Wonderland Studios, Los Angeles; Tarpan Studios, San Rafael; Soundtrack Studios, New York City; Bosstown Recording Studio, Atlanta; Woodland Studio, Nashville, US; SOL Studios, Cookham; the Town House, London; Olympic Studios, London & Wembley Arena London, England
Produced by Barry Beckett, P.M. Dawn, Stuart Epps, Don Henley, Elton John, Nik Kershaw, Steve Lindsey, George Michael, Giorgio Moroder, Greg Penny, Chris Rea, Chris Thomas, Don Was, Narada Michael Walden and Stevie Wonder
Released November 23, 1993
Label The Rocket Record Company, 518 478-2
Highest chart position on release UK 5, US 25

KEY PERSONNEL

Elton John: piano, keyboards, vocals
Dean Parks: guitar (1, 3, 14, 16), lap steel guitar (14)

COVER ART

Brian Aris, Brad Branson, Mark Contratto, Paul Cox, Robert Goldstein, Stephen Harvey, Dominique Issermann, Harry Langdon, Sophie Muller, Hideo Odia, Albert Sanchez, Randee St. Nicholas, Allan Titmuss, Albert Watson and Firooz Zahedi: photography

stuck to the point where, while it steadily went gold in the US (always its chief targeted market), it plateaued at No. 7 in the UK. "Go On and On," he'd sung with Gladys Knight, and he would now do so by transferring his energies into fertile new areas of endeavor. For he was initiating three fields of interest which would change his life. These were: establishing closer ties with Hollywood, the Elton John AIDS Foundation, and meeting David Furnish.

In 2012, Elton told the *Independent* that he'd taken risks during the eighties and considered himself lucky not to have contracted HIV during the tragic AIDS epidemic. After working on the charity single "That's What Friends Are For" with Dionne Warwick and others in '86, he'd taken a growing interest in what could be done to help combat the issues. After performing "Skyline Pigeon" at the funeral of his friend Ryan White in 1990, and being involved in the Freddie Mercury memorials, he wanted to put his fame and contacts book to good use and play an active part. So, in '92 he founded the Elton John AIDS Foundation, a charity aimed at raising money to fund programs for AIDS prevention and to counter prejudice and discrimination against affected individuals. He may or may not have fully known it then, but this was to become a passionate cause of his. One of his major ways of raising both donations and awareness was to host an annual Academy Award party on the night of the Oscars ceremony. It's become a star-studded staple of that scene, and has raised hundreds of millions of dollars.

Celebrity-endorsed as that party is, it's not the only one he hosts for the charity. In the grounds of his sumptuous Old Windsor home he throws the annual White Tie & Tiara Ball, which is another must-attend for all A-listers (royalty, actors, singers) or wannabe A-listers. In 2007, for example, an auction conducted there by Stephen Fry raised millions, with lots including a Rolls Royce and a Tracey Emin original artwork. (To put a cap on the evening, Elton sang "Delilah" with Tom Jones and "Big Spender" with Shirley Bassey.)

1993 was a good year for the previously regularly turbulent love life of the born-again Elton. After multiple failed or fleeting relationships, he met Canadian filmmaker David Furnish. Fifteen years Elton's junior, Furnish was born in Toronto in 1962, and was working for the advertising agency Ogilvy & Mather when appointed to their board in London.

TOP: Elton with Jeanne White, mother of AIDS patient Ryan White, April 1990.
BOTTOM: Elizabeth Taylor, second from right, and Elton, right, are joined on stage by, from left, George Michael, Whoopi Goldberg, and Lionel Richie, for the finale of a concert benefiting the Elizabeth Taylor AIDS Foundation, held at Madison Square Garden, October 11, 1992.

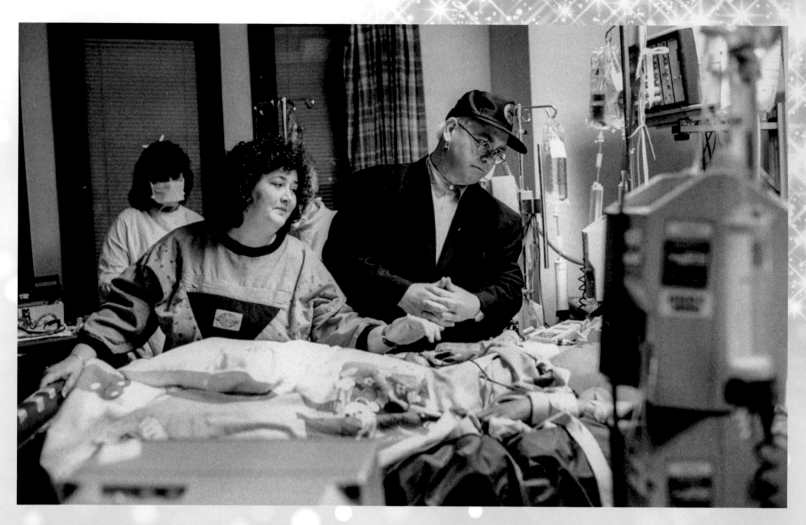

'Partner' is a word that should be preserved for people you play tennis with, or work alongside in business. It doesn't come close to describing the love that I have for David, and he for me. In contrast, 'husband' does.

ELTON JOHN

ABOVE: Elton and David Furnish at the 1995 Golden Globe Awards, Beverly Hills, California.
ABOVE RIGHT: David Furnish and Elton at their Civil Partnership ceremony, Windsor, England, December 21, 2005.
FAR RIGHT: David Furnish, *Tantrums and Tiaras*, 1997.

His fateful meeting with Elton has led to an enduring relationship of a quarter-century and counting. The couple entered into a civil partnership on December 21, 2005—the first day such partnerships were legalized in England—after Elton had proposed six months earlier at their home in Old Windsor. On the ninth anniversary of that date, in 2014, laws having evolved, they converted the civil partnership to marriage, enjoying another ceremony in Windsor. Between those dates they've had two children via surrogacy. Their first, Zachary Jackson Levon Furnish-John, was born in December 2010 in California. In January 2013, second son Elijah Joseph Daniel Furnish-John arrived through the same surrogate.

Furnish has become a successful film producer, and directed the 1997 Elton documentary *Tantrums and Tiaras*, about which more soon. He executive-produced the award-winning *Billy Elliot the Musical*—which debuted on the West End in 2005—for which his husband-to-be wrote the music. It hasn't all been moonlight and roses. In 2008, Elton took some flak for expressing a preference for civil partnerships over marriage for gay people. By 2012, however, he'd changed his view, praising same-sex marriage. "There's a world of difference between calling someone your 'partner' and calling them your 'husband,'" he told the *Independent*. "'Partner' is a word that should be preserved for people you play tennis with, or work alongside in business. It doesn't come close to describing the love that I have for David, and he for me. In contrast, 'husband' does." (Two years later he went further, claiming Jesus would have been in favor of same-sex marriage. In 2010, he'd drawn the ire of the Christian right in America by referring to Jesus as "a compassionate, super-intelligent gay man.")

LEFT: *The Lion King* premiere and party, London, October 7, 1994.
BELOW: Working with lyricist Tim Rice, during *The Lion King* recording, 1994.
RIGHT: Elton performs his Oscar-winning song, "Can You Feel the Love Tonight", at the 67th Annual Academy Awards, Los Angeles, March 27, 1995.
BELOW RIGHT: With Tim Rice, celebrating their Academy Awards, 1995.

In the early and mid-nineties, enjoying the bloom of new romance and detoxed health, Elton was on a roll, becoming something of a Renaissance man. Never mind the Grammys, he was about to bag an Oscar. Along with Tim Rice, he wrote the songs for the epic 1994 Disney animated film *The Lion King*. At the sixty-seventh Academy Awards, three of the five Oscar-nominated songs were from the film. "Can You Feel the Love Tonight" won (and grabbed Elton a Grammy, to boot). "Circle of Life" was also a huge hit, "Hakuna Matata" became a catchphrase, and the soundtrack album topped the *Billboard* charts for nine weeks, eventually selling over fifteen million. "I Just Can't Wait to Be King," suggested another John-Rice song from the score, and Elton did appear to be sitting atop a new throne in the entertainment world. As for the film, the highest-grossing traditionally animated film in history has also been selected for preservation by the US National Film Registry as being "culturally, historically, or aesthetically

LEFT: Elton and Bernie after being inducted into the Rock and Roll Hall of Fame, Cleveland, Ohio, January 19, 1994,

RIGHT: Accepting his Outstanding Contribution to Music Award at the Brit Awards, February 20, 1995,

ELTON JOHN

Made in England

MADE IN ENGLAND

TRACK LIST

Believe
Made in England
House
Cold
Pain
Belfast
Latitude
Please
Man
Lies
Blessed

Recorded at AIR Studios, London, England
Produced by Greg Penny & Elton John
Released March 20, 1995
Label The Rocket Record Company, 526 185-2
Highest chart position on release UK 3, US 13, CAN 3, AUS 6, FRA 2, ITA 4, GER 3, NOR 4, SPA 3, JPN 13

KEY PERSONNEL

Elton John: piano, keyboards, harmonium, lead and backing vocals, string arrangements (9)
Guy Babylon: keyboards, programming, backing vocals (8), string arrangements (9)
Bob Birch: bass guitar, backing vocals (8)
Paul Buckmaster: orchestral arrangements and conductor (1, 3, 4, 6)
Davey Johnstone: guitar, mandolin, banjo, backing vocals (8)
Charlie Morgan: drums

COVER ART

Wherefore Art?: art direction and design
Greg Gorman: photography

significant." A CGI remake is on the way, but *The Lion King* was and remains a pop-culture phenomenon.

If anyone was complaining that Elton John had sold out and gone mainstream (and they were, and he had), this argument was counterbalanced when he was inducted into the Rock and Roll Hall of Fame, on January 19, 1994. His rock and roll credentials were boosted when Axl Rose—a curious choice—presented the honor, saying in his speech: "For myself as well as for many others, no one has been there more for inspiration than Elton John. When we talk of great rock duos like Jimmy Page and Robert Plant, Lennon and McCartney, Mick and Keith—I like to think of Elton John and Bernie Taupin. Also tonight I think Elton should be honored for his great work and contribution in the fight against AIDS. And also his bravery in exposing all the triumphs and tragedies of his personal life." A youthful, healthy-looking, white-clad Elton paid tribute to Winifred Atwell in his acceptance speech.

By 1995, he had added the Brit Awards' Outstanding Contribution to Music accolade to his collection, and enjoyed another top three album with his twenty-fourth studio release, *Made in England*. Dedicated to David Furnish, and co-produced by Elton himself with Greg Penny, it was a full

John-Taupin set of songs, with the title track tapping into their flair for autobiography again, albeit in a more impressionistic style than on the finely detailed *Captain Fantastic*. The title track was no rose-tinted recollection, however, remembering the hard parts of growing up and taking a few choice pot-shots at what Elton and Bernie perceived as the country's failings. The title track hinted at how a love of the piano and Little Richard had got the boy through the days, touching on schoolyard bullying and then the friendship between Elton and Bernie that helped them both feel a sense of belonging. Then there was a dig at, presumably, the *Sun*, and a reference to rising above continued homophobia in England. There's a feeling that the songwriting pair enjoyed a pressure-leavening catharsis venting on this one. "Believe" (which the star performed at the 1995 Brits) was a moderate hit around the world, and its memorable black-and-white video asked us to believe that Elton was flying around New York and London

in a zeppelin. "Belfast" was a love letter to Northern Ireland. The album was the first to feature bassist Bob Birch and was also notable for the return of Paul Buckmaster as orchestral arranger on four tracks, while George Martin arranged "Latitude."

There were, of course, occasional diva tantrums. When a woman had the temerity to wave and call out "Yoo-hoo!" while Elton was playing tennis, he stormed off court in a huff, grumbling, "I'm never coming to the South of France again!" Play resumed as Elton continued his run of collaborations by recording a single, "Live Like Horses," with Luciano Pavarotti.

LEFT: Performing in drag with Kylie Minogue at the Stonewall Equality Show, Royal Albert Hall, London, October 22, 1995.
ABOVE: Elton and Luciano Pavarotti in concert for the War Child charity, Parco Novi Sad, Modena, Italy, June 20, 1996.

The compilation album *Love Songs* went platinum, and early in 1997, Elton celebrated his fiftieth birthday on a high. He certainly didn't dress down for the party he held, living up to expectations by donning a Louis XIV costume. Yet for this Sun King, clouds were on the horizon.

LEFT: Elton with his mother, Sheila, as Queen Elizabeth II, and his stepfather, Fred, as Prince Philip, at his 50th birthday party, Hammersmith Palais, London, April 6, 1997.
BELOW: Elton and David Furnish at the party.

The shocks came brutally. First, fashion guru and close friend Gianni Versace, himself aged fifty, was murdered in Miami Beach on July 15. Six weeks later, on the last day of August, Princess Diana was killed in a Paris car crash. Just thirty-six, she'd been divorced from Prince Charles for one year and three days. Britain and most of the world went into a near-hysterical period of mourning, and her funeral on September 6 at Westminster Abbey was one of the most watched television transmissions ever. Her brother spoke of her "particular brand of magic." The public had fallen in love with their image of her, and Elton had lost a friend with whom he'd bonded over discussing the burdens of vast fame and media invasion. Unforgettably, he performed "Candle in the Wind" at the funeral, the lyrics modified (by Bernie) in tribute to Diana.

"I thought it was very important to project it from a nation's standpoint," explained Bernie. "I wanted to make it like a country singing it. From the first couple of lines I wrote, the rest sort of fell into place . . ." It was the only time Elton had

> **I thought it was very important to project ["Candle in the Wind"] from a nation's standpoint. I wanted to make it like a country singing it.**
>
> BERNIE TAUPIN

LEFT: HRH Princess Diana, Princess of Wales, is greeted by Elton for a charity performance of *Tango Argentino* in aid of National Aids Trust at London's Aldwych Theatre, May 23, 1991.
TOP RIGHT: Elton sings "Candle in the Wind" at the funeral of Diana, Princess of Wales, Westminster Abbey, London, September 6, 1997.
BOTTOM RIGHT: Elton arrives with David Furnish at Princess Diana's funeral at Westminster Abbey.

sung it live, but its impact caught the fevered emotion of the day. Released as a single produced by George Martin with proceeds going to Diana's charities, it rapidly became a must-have item for every household. It now stands as the biggest-selling single since charts began in the fifties. (Some argue that Bing Crosby's "White Christmas," first released in 1942, sold more.) As Elton sang "Goodbye England's rose, may you ever grow in our hearts," a world wept. So huge and all-encompassing was its popularity that its global No. 1 placings and subsequent Grammy and Ivor Novello Awards seemed just inevitable knock-on effects.

Elton was re-energized regarding his charity work, and performed at the Music for Montserrat benefit at the Royal Albert Hall with Paul McCartney, Eric Clapton, Phil Collins, Sting, and others, and participated in the BBC's unlikely but fascinating *Children in Need* version of Lou Reed's "Perfect Day," another No. 1. *The Lion King* musical debuted on Broadway and then in the West End: it was recently cited as the highest earner in box office history (including both theater and film titles). Elton and Tim Rice crafted a follow-up musical for

LEFT: Elton receives Ivor Novello Awards for Best Selling Single, International Hit of the Year, and Best Selling UK Single, Grosvenor House, London, May 28, 1998.
BELOW: Performing with Paul McCartney at the Music for Montserrat concert at the Royal Albert Hall, London, September 15, 1997.

ELTON JOHN

THE BIG PICTURE

THE BIG PICTURE

TRACK LIST

Long Way from Happiness
Live Like Horses
The End Will Come
If the River Can Bend
Love's Got a Lot to Answer For
Something About the Way You Look Tonight
The Big Picture
Recover Your Soul
January
I Can't Steer My Heart Clear of You
Wicked Dreams

Recorded at the Town House and AIR Studios, London, England
Produced by Chris Thomas
Released September 22, 1997
Label The Rocket Record Company, 536 266-2
Highest chart position on release UK 3, US 9, CAN 14, AUS 5, FRA 4, ITA 1, GER 8, NOR 2, SPA 5, JPN 19

KEY PERSONNEL

Elton John: piano, organ, vocals
Guy Babylon: keyboards
Bob Birch: bass guitar
Davey Johnstone: guitars
John Jorgenson: guitars
Charlie Morgan: drums, percussion

COVER ART

Julian Schnabel: painting and photography
Mario Testino: portrait

Disney, *Aida*, based very loosely on Verdi's opera, which won Tony and Grammy awards. Elton tapped into various genres, from reggae to Motown to gospel, and the concept album *Elton John and Tim Rice's Aida*—released in 1999, before the show debuted (and hence before the cast recording)—featured an eclectic array of guests including Janet Jackson, Shania Twain, Spice Girls, and Tina Turner. Another Elton album, *The Big Picture*, had emerged in '97, dedicated to Versace, and while it performed well enough, its presence was overshadowed by the runaway train of "Candle in the Wind 97." There was one more nineties album: *The Muse* was the orchestral score (composed by Elton) for a comedy film starring Albert Brooks (who also directed), Sharon Stone, Andie MacDowell, and Jeff Bridges. The movie flopped, despite Elton singing (Bernie's words) on the title theme.

Elton now had the status and standing to bounce back from a misfire or two. He had plenty to be getting on with. He'd repurchased Watford FC in '97, having sold it ten years before, and became chairman again, a position he held for five years until moving sideways to club president. And having popped up (playing himself) in the Spice Girls movie *Spice World*, as well

as in *The Simpsons* and *South Park* (never let it be said he has no sense of humor), he now released a candid 1997 autobiographical film, directed by someone he trusted: David Furnish. John Reid executive-produced. *Tantrums and Tiaras* followed the star on his mid-nineties *Made in England* tour, layering in interviews and live show excerpts (chiefly from Rio de Janeiro) and overall revealing Elton to be every bit the temperamental prima donna he'd often fessed up to being. We saw him at home, at work, at play. The film is genuinely frank and funny, and for anyone who thought Elton was a complex, almost Jekyll and Hyde character, this provided confirmation. In the film he's sensitive and moody, and spends money like it's going out of fashion. (In 2000, he told the High Court in London that he'd splashed out approximately thirty million pounds in the last two years. That averages out at around £1.5 million per month. Between January '96 and September '97, he admitted to the court,

The press do get you down but I'd rather have that than the adulation and bubble in America.

ELTON JOHN

LEFT: *The Lion King* UK theater premiere, Lyceum Theatre, London, October 19, 1999.
RIGHT: On the the set of *Spice World*, L–R: Victoria Adams, Melanie Chrisholm, Elton, Melanie Brown, Emma Bunton, and Gerry Halliwell, 1997.

ABOVE: In concert in Glasgow, Scotland, December 11, 1997.

RIGHT: Opening the HIV/AIDS Wemroth Wright Ward at St. Mary's Hospital Paddington, London, January 22, 1999.

FAR RIGHT: Receiving his knighthood with his mother, Sheila, partner, David, and stepfather, Fred, Buckingham Palace, London, February 24, 1998.

TO COMMEMORATE THE OFFICIAL
OPENING OF THE REFURBISHED
WEMROTH WRIGHT WARD
BY
SIR ELTON JOHN
ON
22nd JANUARY 1999
THIS REFURBISHMENT WAS MADE POSSIBLE
WITH THE KIND HELP OF GRANTS FROM:
THE ELTON JOHN AIDS FOUNDATION
AND
AIDS CRISIS TRUST

according to the *Independent*, he'd spent almost £10 million on property and—famously—£293,000 on flowers.)

Nobody was keen on giving him a hard time now. He'd proven to the tabloids that he was a tough enemy to make, and his charity work, and the wave of communal emotion around Diana's funeral had established him as a beloved national treasure. In April 1998, he was knighted by Queen Elizabeth II for "services to music and charitable services." Improbably, Reg Dwight was now Sir Elton John. He was the first openly gay musician to receive the honor.

On his seventieth birthday in 2017 he said, "The knighthood gives me fuck all. They're so enamored in America but the English don't care—nothing is sacred in England. I like the irreverence. I like the fact you'll always be shot down if you get too big for your boots. Michael Jackson would never have survived in England. The press do get you down but I'd rather have that than the adulation and bubble in America."

He was more respectful of the title on the day itself, dressing

formally to visit Buckingham Palace and taking his parents as well as David Furnish. "They don't come much bigger than this," he said to the BBC. "I've had a long career and worked hard. But I think the turning point came in 1990 when I got sober, and decided to do some charity work, particularly for the AIDS problem. A knighthood is the icing on the cake." Dropping the humility a degree, he added that the Queen, who knew a thing or two about tiaras, had apologized for interrupting his hectic schedule. "She said I must be terribly busy. But this is not the sort of thing you put off. I flew back from L.A. yesterday and I'm going to Australia on Thursday, but there was no way I would miss this." Glossing over those pugnacious "Made in England" lyrics, he concluded, "I love my country, and to be recognized in such a way—I can't think of anything better."

Elton's 1990s then had come through some body blows but enjoyed some heady triumphs. He had every reason to look forward to the twenty-first century. Arise, Sir Elton.

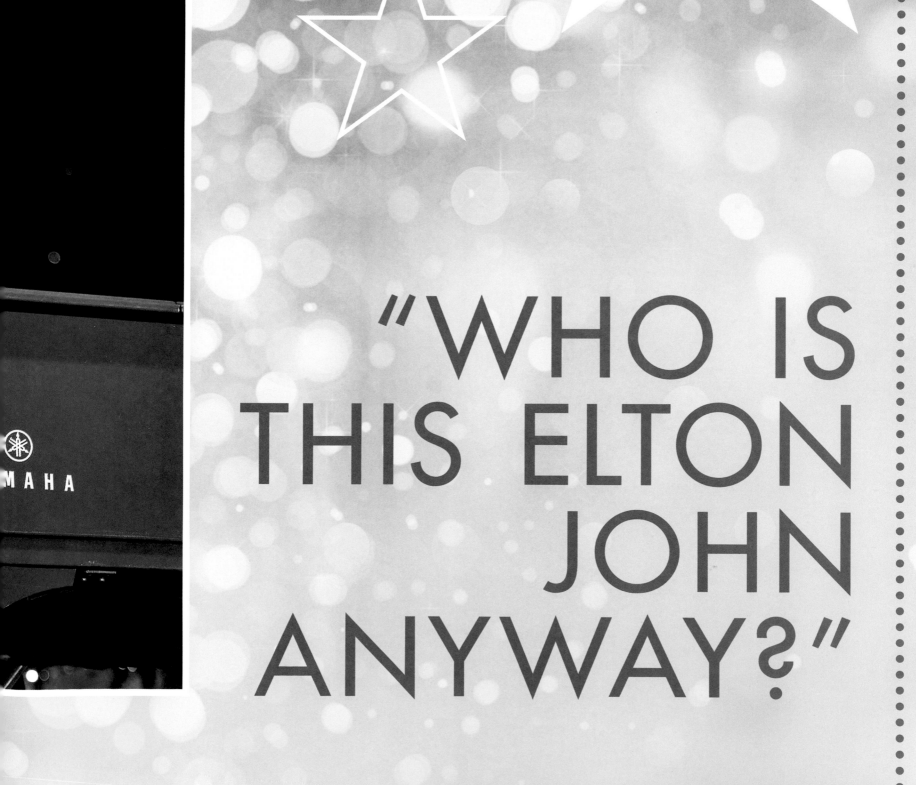

9

"WHO IS THIS ELTON JOHN ANYWAY?"

"If Elton's music makes a fine case that time can stand still, Taupin's lyrics, with their late middle-age perspective, nicely put the lie to that idea."

ENTERTAINMENT WEEKLY

rowing into his fifties, Elton—sorry, Sir Elton—seemed less keen on appearing in his videos. Perhaps old insecurities were flickering again. This wasn't an issue for the two albums he was involved with in 2000. After *The Lion King* he was still in demand in Hollywood, and *The Road to El Dorado* soundtrack accompanied the Dreamworks animated film of the same name. It featured more songs written with Tim Rice and guest appearances by Don Henley, Randy Newman, and the Backstreet Boys. The film bombed, although the John-Rice songs were generally deemed functional, and in some cases, as in the *Rolling Stone* review, proof that "master craftsmanship goes a long way." November saw the release of a happier project as *One Night Only—The Greatest Hits* went gold. Recorded at

Madison Square Garden, it gathered all of Elton's best-known songs and saw friends old and new—Kiki Dee, Ronan Keating, Bryan Adams, Anastasia, Mary J. Blige—joining him onstage. It showed us again that few stars of his stature have been able to work with such a range of artists across all genres as Elton. A DVD offered an extended set.

PREVIOUS PAGE: Performing at the Ahoy Arena in Rotterdam, Netherlands, October 2009.
BELOW LEFT: Performing songs from the movie *The Road to El Dorado* on NBC's *Today Show* at New York's Rockefeller Center, March 2000.
BELOW RIGHT: Elton and Bryan Adams perform at the Greatest Hits concert at Madison Square Garden, October 22, 2000.

ELTON JOHN ONE NIGHT ONLY: THE GREATEST HITS

TRACK LIST

Goodbye Yellow Brick Road
Philadelphia Freedom
Don't Go Breaking My Heart
Rocket Man
Daniel
Crocodile Rock
Sacrifice
Can You Feel the Love Tonight?
Bennie and the Jets
Your Song
Sad Songs (Say So Much)
Candle in the Wind
The Bitch is Back
Saturday Night's Alright (For Fighting)
I'm Still Standing
Don't Let the Sun Go Down on Me
I Guess That's Why They Call It the Blues

Recorded at Madison Square Garden, New York, USA
Produced by Phil Ramone
Released November 13, 2000
Label The Rocket Record Company, 548 334-2
Highest chart position on release UK 7, US 65

KEY PERSONNEL

Elton John: piano, vocals
Davey Johnstone: guitar, vocals
John Jorgenson: guitar, mandolin, pedal steel guitar, saxophone, vocals
Bob Birch: bass guitar, vocals
Guy Babylon: keyboards, vocals
Nigel Olsson: drums, percussion, vocals
Curt Bisquera: drums

COVER ART

David LaChapelle: photography

BELOW: Performing at Albert Dock, Liverpool, England, July 2000.
RIGHT: At the Royal Academy, London, September 2000.

It was, however, the 2001 album *Songs from the West Coast* that clawed back a little more credibility, while again tapping into connections with more topically famous stars. Yet it also touched on his roots. Bernie was in the lyrics seat again, and he and Elton were often actually writing in the same room together. Davey Johnstone was on guitar, and Nigel Olsson returned to the drum stool. Paul Buckmaster was involved, and Stevie Wonder and Billy Preston guested. New collaborators included Táta Vega (who now joined the band) on backing vocals, and cameos by Gary Barlow and Rufus Wainwright. The album was recorded in L.A., and the choice of producer was relatively bold: Patrick Leonard had made his name with Madonna's biggest albums, but his personal tastes were very different to his commercial work with her. Leonard cited Genesis and Pink Floyd as influences and had worked with the latter. He'd played a part in *The Road to El Dorado* soundtrack, and Elton took a chance. This was vindicated: the man behind *Like a Prayer* later

went on to co-write and produce Leonard Cohen's final three albums.

While the three singles were only moderate hits—none made the *Billboard* Hot 100, which ended his run of thirty-one years with at least one song on there—they nonetheless served as high-profile advertisements for the album when their videos became much shown and talked about. With Elton happy to be in them as little as possible ("I fucking hate videos," he told UK television presenter Paul Gambaccini in 2010), other big names lined up to carry them. Robert Downey Jr. lip-synched through "I Want Love," the solitary person in the video, directed by Sam Taylor-Wood. For "This Train Don't Stop There Anymore" (which addressed aging), Justin Timberlake took the role, playing a kind of younger Elton. Paul Reubens—aka Pee-wee Herman—

BELOW LEFT: At the Ritz, Piccadilly, London, August 2001.
BELOW: With video director Sam Taylor-Wood, Los Angeles, March 2001.

SONGS FROM THE WEST COAST

TRACK LIST

The Emperor's New Clothes
Dark Diamond
Look Ma, No Hands
American Triangle
Original Sin
Birds
I Want Love
The Wasteland
Ballad of the Boy in the Red Shoes
Love Her Like Me
Mansfield
This Train Don't Stop There Anymore

Recorded at Ocean Way Studios, Los Angeles, USA
Produced by Patrick Leonard
Released October 1, 2001
Label The Rocket Record Company, 586 330-2
Highest chart position on release UK 2, US 15, CAN 9, AUS 7, FRA 19, ITA 3, GER 14, NOR 2, SPA 21, JPN 68

PERSONNEL

Elton John: piano, harmonium, vocals
Rusty Anderson: electric guitar, bouzouki
Gary Barlow: backing vocals
Jay Bellerose: percussion
Paul Buckmaster: horn and string arrangements, conductor
Paul Bushnell: bass guitar, backing vocals
Matt Chamberlain: drums, percussion
David Channing: acoustic guitar, dobro
Bruce Gaitsch: acoustic guitar
Davey Johnstone: acoustic guitar, electric guitar, mandolin, backing vocals
Kudisan Kai: backing vocals
Patrick Leonard: Hammond B3 organ, Mellotron, keyboards
Nigel Olsson: drums, backing vocals
Billy Preston: Hammond B3 organ
Tata Vega: backing vocals
Rufus Wainwright: harmony vocals on "American Triangle"
Stevie Wonder: clavinet, harmonica on "Dark Diamond"

COVER ART

Sam Taylor-Wood: photography

> "[The] spirit and ambition [of his music] have finally come back home."
>
> *ROLLING STONE*

was a risqué choice to play John Reid. And for "Original Sin," Elton did briefly appear, in unflattering football kit and baseball cap, playing the role of Elizabeth Taylor's husband, with Mandy Moore as their daughter. Moore plays a young seventies Elton fan, who drifts into a dream of attending one of his shows, where she hangs out with lookalikes of his period celebrity pals: Barbra Streisand, Liza Minnelli, Cher, Bette Midler. She's an ecstatic Alice through the looking glass.

All this shrewd referencing of Elton's early glory years and cross-branding with a new generation of pop stars helped boost an album that was warmly received on its own terms. While surprisingly struggling in the States, it was a UK No. 2. Many praised his return to his earlier sound, and Elton, citing Ryan Adams's recent *Heartbreaker* as an inspiration, was proud to have used analog tape. The song "American Triangle" was about Matthew Shepard, a gay college student who'd been murdered in 1998. Overall the album felt as if its heart was in the right

place, even if the songs—and Bernie's lyrics misfired in parts—weren't as strong as the production and videos needed them to be. To consolidate, another compilation—*Greatest Hits 1970–2002*, a three-CD set—came out a year later, with Universal now owning Polygram. It went platinum.

After the horrors of 9/11, Elton appeared at the Concert for New York City, the benefit held at Madison Square Garden, performing "I Want Love" and a duet with Billy Joel on "Your Song." He and Joel were to develop a friendship and sometime touring partnership. Elton's profile on the pop charts experienced another pleasantly surprising recharge when "Are You Ready for Love?," a song recorded during the 1977 Thom Bell sessions in Philadelphia, suddenly rose from footnote to full-on ubiquitously enjoyed smash. An Ashley Beedle remix helped, as did a retro seventies-disco video, and perhaps most of all the use of the track in a major TV ad campaign for the new football season on Sky Sports. Elton's fifth British No. 1,

Elton John Peachtree Road

PEACHTREE ROAD

TRACK LIST
Weight of the World
Porch Swing in Tupelo
Answer in the Sky
Turn the Lights Out When You Leave
My Elusive Drug
They Call Her the Cat
Freaks in Love
All That I'm Allowed
I Stop and I Breathe
Too Many Tears
It's Getting Dark in Here
I Can't Keep This from You

Recorded at Tree Studios & Silent Sound, Atlanta; the Record Plant, Los Angeles, USA
Produced by Elton John
Released November 9, 2004
Label Mercury, 9867611
Highest chart position on release UK 21, US 17

KEY PERSONNEL
Elton John: piano, Fender Rhodes, lead and backing vocals
Davey Johnstone: acoustic guitar, electric guitar, slide guitar, baritone guitar, Leslie, sitar, dobro, mandolin, backing vocals
Nigel Olsson: drums, backing vocals
Guy Babylon: Hammond organ, piano, Fender Rhodes, programming
Bob Birch: bass guitar, backing vocals
John Mahon: percussion, backing vocals
John Jorgenson: pedal steel guitar

COVER ART
Sam Taylor-Wood: photography

it reconfirms how lithe and likeable Bell's sunny grooves were. There was another album before John made his next major foray into musical theater. *Peachtree Road*, his twenty-seventh, was named after the street in Atlanta, Georgia, where Elton had one of his (then) four homes. Mostly recorded nearby in January 2004, it's the only album throughout his lengthy career where he's credited as sole producer. Sam Taylor-Wood took the cover photo, but it's of a nearby suburb instead of the Peachtree Road area itself, as she considered the latter too busy to fit the music's reflective mood. The country rock flavors drew good reviews but commercially it was a relative failure. Poignantly, it

LEFT: Elton and Billy Joel perform at the Concert for New York, Madison Square Garden, October 20, 2001.
ABOVE: Elton's waxwork is prepared for display at Madame Tussaud's, New York, June 2003.

LEFT: Elton and David Furnish leave the Guildhall, Windsor, after their Civil Ceremony, December 21, 2005.
RIGHT: Elton joins the cast of *Billy Elliot* for a curtain call at the Victoria Palace Theatre, London, May 2005.

was dedicated to Gus and Sheila Dudgeon, the producer who'd facilitated Elton's big career breakthrough having very sadly died with his wife in a car accident in 2002.

Truth was, the fate of individual albums was not so crucial to Elton now. He was a carved-in-stone household name, entertainment royalty, to whom one-off hits or misses were irrelevant. Besides, his return to the world of musical theater brought riotously rich pickings. Composing music for an adaptation of *Billy Elliot*, the 2000 film set in 1980s County Durham, with lyrics and book by Lee Hall (who'd written the film), he probably knew they were backing a winner, but, born to boogie, it danced like its legs were on fire. *Billy Elliot the*

Musical opened at London's Victoria Palace Theatre in 2005, and after gushing reviews won both multiple awards and the hearts of the public. It would soon boast four Olivier Awards, including Best New Musical, and became the eleventh-longest-running musical in West End history until closing in April 2016 after 4,566 performances. After productions on Broadway (where it won a Tony for Best Musical, as well as nine more Tonys in other categories), and in Sydney, Chicago, Toronto, São Paolo, and other major cities (and tours) it's been seen by over eleven million people worldwide. Its gross? Around $800 million. Trading boxing gloves for ballet shoes was rarely so profitable. All this with songs called "Merry Christmas Maggie

Thatcher," "Grandma's Song," and, perhaps more key to its themes, "Expressing Yourself."

It wasn't as if Elton needed the money. When *Billy Elliot* debuted, he was in the middle of a massive residency at the Colosseum at Caesars Palace in Las Vegas. Contracted in October 2003 to play seventy-five shows over three years, he was putting on a memorable spectacle entitled *The Red Piano*, a multimedia concert with props and video montages designed by in-vogue photographer-director David LaChapelle. Vegas had its seasons covered: when Elton was off duty, Celine Dion took over the Palace, the pair alternating runs of shows. In the end, after some cancellations and rescheduling, *The Red Piano* stayed upright until 2009. A similar show was taken on tour around the world. For all the state-of-the-art visuals, the set list took few risks, giving the people what they wanted, smartly rattling through Elton's best-known seventies and eighties hits.

A couple of these old songs had already found a second life and put Elton, who'd struggled to get a No. 1 for so long, atop the British charts twice more. "Sorry Seems to Be the Hardest Word" had been revived just before Christmas in 2002 when boy band Blue covered it with Elton guesting: another sign of his knack of being in the right place at the right time, and credibility be damned. There was a more streetwise offering in January 2005 when a posthumous single from East Coast rapper Tupac (2-Pac) Shakur, "Ghetto Gospel," topped the UK charts for three weeks. It took an affecting sample from "Indian Sunset," which had appeared back in 1971 on *Madman Across the Water*. Paying tribute to murdered black activists Malcolm X and Bobby Hutton, it was the polar opposite to Blue's confection and a pleasingly strange place for the old Elton track to show up all these years on. Although the original album version did not include the sample, its producer was Eminem, whose own relationship with Elton was to twist and turn under the glare of publicity.

Elton told *Rolling Stone* that he wanted to work with Pharrell Williams, Timbaland, Snoop Dogg, and Kanye West, as well as with Eminem. Such a plan never fully materialized, and his being granted the title of Disney Legend by the film corporation wasn't too down with the kids. When Elton showed willing by inviting rebel du jour Pete Doherty of the Libertines and Babyshambles onstage at Live 8 at Hyde Park in July 2005 for a rendition of T. Rex's "Children of the Revolution" (Elton having already safely played his own rockier numbers "The Bitch Is Back" and "Saturday Night's Alright"), the post-show discussion was all about how not-with-the-program Doherty had seemed.

Backstage at the Red Piano residency, the Colosseum at Caesars Palace, Las Vegas, February 2004.

THE CAPTAIN & THE KID

TRACK LIST
Postcards from Richard Nixon
Just Like Noah's Ark
Wouldn't Have You Any Other Way (NYC)
Tinderbox
And the House Fell Down
Blues Never Fade Away
The Bridge
I Must Have Lost It on the Wind
Old 67
The Captain and The Kid

Recorded at Center Staging, Atlanta, USA
Produced by Elton John & Matt Still
Released September 18, 2006
Label Mercury, 1706422
Highest chart position on release UK 6, US 18, AUS 37, FRA 56, GER 25, NOR 10, SPA 52

KEY PERSONNEL
Elton John: vocals, piano
Davey Johnstone: guitar, banjo, mandolin, harmonica, backing vocals
Nigel Olsson: drums, backing vocals
Guy Babylon: keyboards
Bob Birch: bass guitar, backing vocals
John Mahon: percussion, backing vocals
Matt Still: backing vocals
Arthur: "woof-bells"

COVER ART
David Costa: art direction and design
Ryan McGinley: photography

Elton's best album in decades.
"

ENTERTAINMENT WEEKLY

So, the next tactic was to go back to the future. The album *The Captain & the Kid*, released in September 2006, found Bernie and Elton excavating autobiography again. Picking up (in theory, even if it was at times nebulous) where *Captain Fantastic and the Brown Dirt Cowboy* left off in 1975, it examined the ups and downs in the writing pair's lives over the last three decades of success, self-abuse, and resurgence. Hopes were high for this, but Interscope Records elected not to release a single and to pitch it as a grandiose complete work, with Elton and Bernie looking overly earnest on the cover as they stared at, respectively, a piano and a horse—emphasizing their contrasts. It's a faintly elegiac exercise, which, for all its self-regard, has some moving passages. "Postcards from Richard Nixon" opened with a bubbly love letter to Americana, while "Just Like Noah's Ark" and "Wouldn't Have You Any Other Way (NYC)" also recalled hot and hedonistic times Stateside. The piano pleas of "The Bridge" were—perhaps deliberately—reminiscent of "Your Song," and elsewhere there were memories of the erosion of innocence and fallen friends, from John Lennon to AIDS victims. "Blues Never Fade Away" is touching in its honesty, as Elton (via Bernie's lines) marvels at how fortunate he's been to survive and thrive through all his misguided, risky excesses.

Some critics suggested that the John-Taupin efforts to reclaim their seventies glory days were perhaps too self-conscious now, and that they'd long ago lost their handle on it. Others loved the album's nostalgic, old-fashioned analog sound and appreciated the purity of intention. "Elton's best album in decades," said *Entertainment Weekly*. "If Elton's music makes a fine case that time can stand still, Taupin's lyrics, with their late middle-age

In concert on the Captain and the Kid tour, Nassau Coliseum, New York, November 2006.

perspective, nicely put the lie to that idea." For all that, the record didn't sell well. Disillusioned, he didn't make another solo studio album for seven years: an astonishingly long period given his lifelong penchant for the prolific. One can assume the album and its personal tales meant a lot to him, and its commercial failure stung.

There was another blow to Elton's and Bernie's egos, if not confidence, when they experienced what can only be described as a dramatic disaster. Without Tim Rice, they wrote the songs for *Lestat*, a musical inspired by Anne Rice's *The Vampire Chronicles*, with book written by Linda Woolverton. Vampires were all the rage. It seemed like a surefire hit. Unfortunately, this tale of a gay vampire, after a premiere in San Francisco, ran for just thirty-nine performances on Broadway in spring 2006. The cast recording album was never released. "Bloody awful,"

said the *New York Post*. "Just deadly," quipped another review. The *New York Times* deemed the songs "pulpy and mostly interchangeable." In terms of Elton's canon of work, *Lestat* has likely been buried deep in the cellars of some distant, fog-shrouded Transylvanian castle.

As ever, the Elton John fairground ride was bigger than one project or one album, and, undead, the circus rode on. For his sixtieth birthday in March 2007, he played Madison Square Garden, his home away from home, for the sixtieth time—a record. Robin Williams and Whoopi Goldberg appeared onstage and, unusually, there were even a few words from Bernie. The show was broadcast live and a DVD, directed by David Mallet, ensued, as well as yet another "definitive" (its own adjective) greatest hits compilation, the platinum-selling *Rocket Man*. That July, Elton inevitably starred at the Concert for Diana at Wembley Stadium, in memory of his late friend and in honor of what would have been her forty-sixth birthday. He opened and closed the show, with hosts Prince William and Prince Harry looking on, proceeds going to charity. Between Elton's two brief sets, everyone from Duran Duran, Bryan Ferry, and Rod Stewart to Take That, Pharrell, and Kanye West

LEFT: The Rocket Man tour, Boardwalk Hall, Atlantic City, New Jersey, July 19, 2008.
ABOVE: Celebrating his 60th birthday with a record-breaking 60th concert at Madison Square Garden in New York. Helping him celebrate are Bernie Taupin, Whoopi Goldberg, and Robin Williams, March 25, 2007.

email to Elton explaining that he was an important influence on them. He told *Entertainment Weekly* that Elton had been touched, and enthusiastic. "In the studio he was very relaxed and gracious, and he's got a great sense of humor. We were just trying to be cool: 'Oh yeah, no big deal.' But we were excited! The drummer and I had to walk out a couple of times to smoke cigarettes, going, 'Holy shit, this is killer.' It's one of those highlights you can't expect in life, and you're lucky to get once in a while." Their surprise idol commented, "I never thought I'd play on an Alice in Chains record. When I heard the song I really wanted to do it. I liked the fact that it was so beautiful and simple. They had a great idea of what they wanted me to do on it and it turned out great."

He didn't do it for the session fee. Tales of his riches and extravagance continued to appear. He now had numerous homes—Old Windsor of course, but also Atlanta, Los Angeles, Venice, Nice, and another London pad in upmarket Holland Park. His passion for art had grown to the point where he had one of the most impressive private photography collections in the world. The dazzling exhibition *The Radical Eye: Modernist Photography from the Sir Elton John Collection* was to run across late 2016 and early 2017 at Tate Modern, and included portraits of Matisse, Picasso, and Breton, and works by Brassaï, Dorothea Lange, and Rodchenko). On top of this, he'd sold twenty cars (Jaguars, Ferraris, Bentleys, Rolls Royces) in 2001 for a couple of million pounds, saying he was out of the country too often to have the fun of driving them. There was a 2003 Sotheby's sale of the contents of the Holland Park home (so that he could refurbish and hang some of that art collection), and he now annually sold off clothes he no longer fancied, for charity, via two shops, one in New York named Elton's Closet, and London's Out of the Closet.

Elton is well known for, and highly adept at, forging friendships with other stars from any generation, and one of his most unlikely bloomed after inauspicious beginnings. He's been good pals with rapper Eminem since he duetted with him at the 2001 Grammys, on the controversial hip-hopper's song "Stan." At the time, Eminem was getting much criticism for what seemed to be homophobia in his lyrics. He asked Elton to guest with him, but then claimed he didn't know about Elton's sexuality. "I didn't know he was gay. I didn't know anything about his personal life. I didn't really care," he told MTV. "But being that he was gay, and he had my back, I think it made a statement in itself, saying that he understood where I was coming from." Even so, Elton backed him up, telling Zane Lowe: "For me, Eminem was never homophobic. I listened to the whole of the *Marshall Mathers* album while driving to a show, and was floored by it. And I thought, how could anyone think this is . . . he's just writing about things the way they are. Not

appeared. Speakers on the day included Nelson Mandela, Bill Clinton, and Tony Blair.

All this while the stop-start *The Red Piano* tour played on in parallel to distinct tour dates, and as soon as it finally climaxed in Vegas in 2009, Elton announced a tour with Billy Joel. The rocket man and the piano man pooled their (surely overlapping) demographics for another money-spinner. Their *Face to Face* tour had recurred through the mid-nineties, and they seemed to enjoy mingling their sets, albeit with each getting extended solo spots.

There was a less-celebrated but more unusual team-up that year when Elton played piano on a song by Seattle grunge-rockers Alice in Chains. The track, "Black Gives Way to Blue," was a tribute to the band's late lead singer, Layne Staley, for whom an Elton John gig had been the first live show he'd attended. Alice in Chains founder Jerry Cantrell had written an

how he thinks, but the way they are."

Not everybody agreed, but the pair stayed genuine friends. Later in the decade, when Eminem was struggling with drug addiction, Elton, who knew a thing or two about rehab—and had of course counseled other celebs—gave him supportive advice. The rapper told the *Guardian* in 2009: "When I first wanted to get sober, I called Elton. . . . He's somebody who's in the business and can identify and relate to the lifestyle and how hectic things can be. He understands the pressures, and any other reasons that you want to come up with for doing drugs. I reached out to him and told him, 'Look, I'm going through a problem and I need your advice . . .'"

The one-time wild piano man was now Sir Elton, warm, avuncular music industry safety net and dispenser of paternal advice for younger stars with hungry appetites for self-destruction. Unexpectedly—the guy behind *The Lion King* bonds with the guy behind *8 Mile*—his friendship with Eminem has persisted, the pair more recently chatting on the phone

(for publication by *Interview* magazine) and expressing their love for each other. "I love you too," says Eminem, after Elton's said, "Your sobriety day is in my diary. I'm just so proud of you." Significantly, Elton is still able to confront Eminem when the rapper lapses back into homophobic lyrics, and Eminem generally apologizes. Progress, of sorts. And so, Elton's own invincible progression continued into the present decade.

LEFT: David Furnish with some of Elton's Versace costumes from *The Muppet Show* at the Out of the Closet charity shop, London, November 2002.
ABOVE: Elton and Eminem after performing a duet at the 43rd Annual Grammy Awards, Staples Center, Los Angeles, February 21, 2001.

10

FAREWELL YELLOW BRICK ROAD

"I don't have to make pop records any more. I thought: the world isn't screaming for another Elton John record, and I'm not screaming for it either unless it's going to be different. In the '70s, '80s and '90s, the record companies always said we had to have a single, and I think I fulfilled my brief. But at 63, the singles chart isn't one I'm going to be in very often. To me now, it's all about writing albums and trying to be mature."

ELTON JOHN

If Eminem was an odd friendship for Elton to embark upon, an even more peculiar one flickered when he played at the fourth wedding of Rush Limbaugh. Limbaugh was and is a conservative political commentator and talk show host, whose guests at the Palm Beach ceremony on June 6, 2010 included Rudy Giuliani, Sean Hannity, and Karl Rove. The extremely rich Limbaugh has a huge audience, to whom he lambasts liberals. By now it was becoming clear that Elton wasn't choosing his network of alliances based on his own apparently more progressive leanings.

He'd begun the new decade with a more logical team-up, duetting at January's Grammy Awards show with Lady Gaga, his first Grammy stage–share stint since the one with Eminem in 2001. They gamely rattled through her song "Speechless" and his evergreen chestnut "Your Song." In a nod to her then-outrageous fashion choices, his face and suit were artfully daubed with dirt.

"I don't have to make pop records any more," he told Paul Gambaccini as he launched *The Union*, a collaboration with Leon Russell, which marked a new chapter in his album catalog. "I thought: the world isn't screaming for another Elton John record, and I'm not screaming for it either unless it's going to be different. In the '70s, '80s and '90s, the record companies always said we had to have a single, and I think I fulfilled my brief. But at 63, the singles chart isn't one I'm going to be in

PREVIOUS PAGE: Performing at the Apple Music Festival, the Roundhouse, London, September 18, 2016.
BELOW: Elton and Lady Gaga perform at the 52nd Annual Grammy Awards, Staples Center, Los Angeles, January 31, 2010.

very often. To me now, it's all about writing albums and trying to be mature." Describing Russell as his idol and working with him as "a humbling, moving experience," he revealed that he'd had the idea after digging deep into Russell's music while remembering their American touring days together forty years before. If Russell's name had faded since then, and his health wasn't good, Elton hoped this brush with the limelight might reignite people's interest in the Oklahoma-born country-blues man, who had played keyboards for Phil Spector and the Beach Boys, as well as writing songs such as "Superstar," "This Masquerade," and "A Song for You" (all made famous by the Carpenters), and "Delta Lady" (popularized by Joe Cocker). "There's no point doing this record if it doesn't bring his work to light," said Elton. "I want him to be comfortable financially. I want to improve his life a little." (He seems perhaps to have underestimated how many records the Carpenters sold.) To this aim the pair had worked with Bernie Taupin again (most songs were John-Taupin compositions) and hired the esteemed T Bone Burnett as producer, calling in A-list guest appearances from Brian Wilson, Booker T. Jones, Don Was, and Neil Young. With songs recorded in one or two takes, it had a rootsy, near-gospel feel. It rose into the top three in the US (its chief demographic), hovering just outside the Top 10 in the UK. Reviews were rosy, and *Rolling Stone* rated it as 2010's third-best album. Russell was inducted into the Rock and Roll Hall of Fame the following year. He died in 2016, aged 74.

Pausing for barely a moment, Elton opened his new Las Vegas show *The Million Dollar Piano* at Caesars Palace in September 2011. This intermittent residency ran for three years, and included, that October, his three-thousandth live concert. He still found time to play his first shows in Costa Rica. And another fascinating team-up saw him providing guest vocals on Kate Bush's album *50 Words for Snow*, trading vocals with her on "Snowed In at Wheeler Street."

June 2012 saw the Queen's Diamond Jubilee, and the celebrations included the Diamond Jubilee Concert held on the Mall outside Buckingham Palace. Windsor favorite Sir Elton was there of course, singing "Your Song," "Crocodile Rock," and—perhaps as a deferential dedication to Her Majesty—"I'm Still Standing." The royals also rattled their jewelry to the swinging sounds of Paul McCartney, Stevie Wonder, Robbie Williams, Gary Barlow, Tom Jones, Cliff Richard, and many others, perhaps least expectedly Grace Jones. Elton pushed on with charity shows in Ukraine with Queen and Adam Lambert, and found himself on a No. 1 album without lifting a finger, as a remix album—*Good Morning to the Night*, dished

TOP: Elton and Leon Russell in concert, Beacon Theatre, New York, October 19, 2010.
LEFT: Elton and Leon Russell in the studio, 2011.

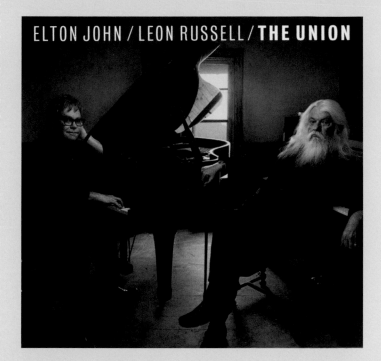

THE UNION

TRACK LIST

If It Wasn't for Bad
Eight Hundred Dollar Shoes
Hey Ahab
Gone to Shiloh
Jimmie Rodgers' Dream
There's No Tomorrow
Monkey Suit
The Best Part of the Day
A Dream Come True
When Love Is Dying
I Should Have Sent Roses
Hearts Have Turned to Stone
Never Too Old (To Hold Somebody)
In the Hands of Angels

Recorded at the Village, Los Angeles, USA
Produced by T Bone Burnett
Released October 19, 2010
Label Mercury, 2750475
Highest chart position on release UK 12, US 3, CAN 7, AUS 28, FRA 51, ITA 28, GER 23, NOR 5, SPA 30

KEY PERSONNEL
Elton John: vocals (1–15), piano (2–4, 6–15)
Leon Russell: piano, vocals; BGV arrangement (1, 5, 7, 10, 16)
Jim Keltner: drums & percussion (1–9, 11–15)
Jay Bellerose: drums & percussion (1–15)
Dennis Crouch: acoustic bass (1–4, 6–10, 12–15)
Marc Ribot: guitar (1–4, 6, 7, 9, 10, 13–15), acoustic guitar (8)
T Bone Burnett: electric guitar (3, 6, 12)

COVER ART
Peacock: design
Frank W. Ockenfels, Joseph Guay, Annie Leibovitz and Steve Todoroff: photography

Performing at the
Rock in Rio concert,
Rio De Janeiro,
September 23,
2011.

up by Australian dance outfit Pnau—caught the popular taste. Using samples from old Elton tracks to rustle up new grooves, it was an unmitigated success. Pnau, wrote the *Guardian*'s Phil Mongredien, "have been mentored by Elton for five years, and it's with his blessing that they have reimagined his early '70s output by splicing together snippets of songs to create something wholly new and oddly affecting. Refreshingly unpredictable, this is a blueprint for what remix albums should aspire to." Buoyed by this proximity to topicality, Elton opened 2013 with yet another Grammy Awards–ceremony team-up with the hot act of the day. It was becoming a tradition. This time it was Ed Sheeran who was emailing his lyrics to Elton, as they sang Sheeran's hit "The A Team," soon after Taylor Swift had opened the show. It would have been gratifying to Elton that he was still respected across the generations: from Leon Russell to Ed Sheeran is quite a stretch.

LEFT: Elton and Ed Sheeran perform together at the 55th Annual Grammy Awards, Staples Center, Los Angeles, February 10, 2013.
ABOVE: Elton performs at a concert to celebrate being awarded the first Brits Icon Award, London Palladium, London, September 2, 2013.

Elton next guested on piano and vocals on the track "Fairweather Friends" from the new Queens of the Stone Age album, *Like Clockwork*. He even said it was him who'd called (QOTSA front man) Josh Homme, asking if he could play with them, after enjoying Homme's side project Them Crooked Vultures. Clearly, Elton was still the obsessive records fan he'd been since his teenage days. As such he'd have accepted the first ever Brits Icon award at the September 2013 Brits with pride and glee. Especially as his old chum Rod Stewart made the presentation, onstage at the London Palladium. The pair then spiritedly sang "Sad Songs (Say So Much)" together. The same month saw the release of Elton's twenty-ninth studio album, even if he didn't have to make pop records any more.

With T Bone Burnett again on the production desk, *The Diving Board*, recorded in L.A., eschewed the use of Elton's regular band members. Burnett had urged a return to the simple piano/bass/drums setup of Elton's past, and the songs (lyrics by Bernie) were written in just a couple of days. The singer hailed it as the most exciting solo record he'd made "in a long, long time," but its announced release date was twice postponed, because, according to *Rolling Stone*, Elton was dissatisfied and wanted to

THE DIVING BOARD

TRACK LIST

Oceans Away
Oscar Wilde Gets Out
A Town Called Jubilee
The Ballad of Blind Tom
Dream # 1
My Quicksand
Can't Stay Alone Tonight
Voyeur
Home Again
Take This Dirty Water
Dream # 2
The New Fever Waltz
Mexican Vacation (Kids in the Candlelight)
Dream # 3
The Diving Board

Recorded at the Village, Los Angeles, USA
Produced by T Bone Burnett
Released September 13, 2013
Label Mercury, 3743912
Highest chart position on release UK 3, US 4, CAN 7,
AUS 26, FRA 24, ITA 12, GER 11, NOR 10, SPA 36

KEY PERSONNEL
Elton John: piano, vocals (1–4, 6–10, 12, 13, 15)
Jay Bellerose: drums (2, 3, 4, 6–10, 12–15)
Raphael Saadiq: bass guitar (2, 3, 4, 6, 7, 8, 10, 12–15)
Keefus Ciancia: keyboards (2, 3, 4, 6–10, 12)

COVER ART
Mat Maitland: art direction
Tim Barber: photography

write some new songs for it. Taupin even declared that the title had been changed to "Voyeur" (the name of another track), but somewhere along the way it changed back. Somewhat revised, it surfaced with Elton now calling it "my most adult album." Titles included "Oscar Wilde Gets Out," "A Town Called Jubilee," and "My Quicksand," Bernie serving up his usual blend of sentiment and cynicism. *The Diving Board* leaped into the top three in both the US and UK, Elton's highest American chart placing since 1976's *Blue Moves*. Among all the generic "true return to form" reviews from publications, *Rolling Stone* reckoned Elton had "regained his sense of musical possibility and taken a brave, graceful jump." Robert Hilburn, the man whose praise for John's American debut at the Troubadour in 1970 had started this whole crazy ball rolling, said that if these songs had been performed there back then, he'd have been equally "showered with applause and acclaim."

Perhaps now content that he could still make pop records if the fancy struck, Elton took a brief break from his music career. The year 2014 wound up as a momentous one in his personal life, as on December 21, eight months after gay marriage was legalized in England, he and David Furnish—his civil partner for nine years to the day—married in Windsor. Their two sons, Zachary and Elijah, as previously discussed, had arrived via surrogate in 2010 and 2013. He'd had his now-customary controversies before marrying David: in 2013 he'd been pressured to boycott Russia because of its "gay propaganda" law but played there anyway, telling his Moscow audience that the laws were "inhumane and isolating" and that he was "deeply saddened and shocked by the current legislation." Unexpectedly, Elton's approach seemed to have an effect. Self-proclaimed tough guy President Vladimir Putin responded with an olive branch, saying there was no anti-gay discrimination in his country, and even declaring, "Elton John—he's an extraordinary person, a distinguished musician, and millions of our people sincerely love him, regardless of his sexual orientation." Emboldened, Elton offered to introduce Putin to Russian people abused under the president's laws banning "homosexual propaganda." Matters were confused by prank callers, who got through to Elton pretending to be Putin, and the singer thanked the Russian leader for "his" call on Instagram. Eventually, in September 2015, Putin did call to invite him to a meeting to discuss LBGT rights in Russia.

Back at the day job, another "pop record," his thirtieth solo studio album and his most recent, arrived. *Wonderful Crazy Night*, a February 2016 release, was again recorded in L.A. and co-produced by Elton with T Bone Burnett. It regrouped the old

Elton and David with their sons, Zachary and Elijah, at Watford Football Club, December 2014.

LEFT: Stevie Nicks performs at the Elton John AIDS Foundation's 11th Annual An Enduring Vision benefit, Cipriani Wall Street, New York, October 15, 2012.
RIGHT: Hillary Clinton joins Elton at the 12th Annual AIDS Foundation benefit, Cipriani Wall Street, New York, October 15, 2013.
BELOW: David Furnish and Elton at the 13th Annual AIDS Foundation benefit, Cipriani Wall Street, New York, October 28, 2014.

> **"There's a bit more gravel and grit in his voice these days."**
>
> *GUARDIAN*

band (as far as mortality allowed) for the first time in a decade, with Davey Johnstone, Nigel Olsson, and Ray Cooper featuring. Bernie, of course, wrote all the lyrics again. The Captain and the Kid had proven to be a resilient team. Hosting singles such as "Looking Up," the title track, and "Blue Wonderful," it was to be a Top 10 album in most countries, with reviewers kind. The *Guardian* thought it "succeeds in recreating the rootsy Americana of his youth" and suggested that the reboot with Leon Russell had done him a power of good. "There's a bit more gravel and grit in his voice these days." A year later there was yet another greatest hits collection, *Diamonds*, and that's where the Elton John discography to date rests. (There were two tribute albums released in April 2018, *Revamp* and *Restoration*. The former ("the pop one") was driven by Elton whereas the latter ("the country one") was seen as Bernie's project. Elton spoke highly of these, "thrilled" and "humbled" by the contributions from the likes of Coldplay ("We All Fall in Love Sometimes"), Lady Gaga ("Your Song"), Ed Sheeran ("Candle in the Wind")

LEFT: Performing on the Diving Board tour at Joe Louis Arena, Detroit, Michigan, November 29, 2013.
RIGHT: American tennis star Andy Roddick takes a selfie with, from left: Billie Jean King, Tim Henman, Kim Clijsters, Jamie Murray, Martina Hingis, Elton, Heather Watson, and John McEnroe at the 22nd Mylan World Team Tennis Smash Hits, Royal Albert Hall, London, December 17, 2014. The event raises money for the Elton John AIDS Foundation.
BELOW: Elton meets US Secretary of State, John Kerry, to discuss the work of the Elton John AIDS Foundation, Washington, DC, October 24, 2014.

and Miley Cyrus ("Don't Let the Sun Go Down on Me") on *Revamp*. He described Bernie's list of country performers on *Restoration* as "astonishing . . . both new and legendary": these included Don Henley and Vince Gill ("Sacrifice"), Kacey Musgraves ("Roy Rogers") and Willie Nelson ("Border Song"). Miley Cyrus managed to appear on both albums, bringing her own persona to "The Bitch Is Back" here.

If Elton's recording schedule was on pause, he was as ever busy playing vast concerts (like Hyde Park in 2016 for Radio 2) and unshirking in his support of AIDS-related charities. Light relief came as he took an acting role in the 2017 hit spy-comedy movie *Kingsman: The Golden Circle*. The acting wasn't a huge stretch: he played himself, or rather a caricature of the Elton John persona. He's kidnapped by Julianne Moore's character, and forced to sing for her, but helps to destroy her aggressive robot dogs. OK, this sequel to a box office success is not *Citizen Kane*, but it's not every week you get to be in a film with Colin Firth and Jeff Bridges. And the film's lead, young Welshman Taron Egerton, was soon to play an English hero even more beloved than Eddie the Eagle, who he'd recreated in a movie that same year. Egerton was to land the plum role of Elton himself. We'll come to that.

There was talk in early 2017 of Elton getting back into musical theater, with reports that he'd be writing the score for a Broadway production of the 2006 film *The Devil Wears Prada*. That project remains mysterious at present. In June, the award-winning documentary series *The American Epic Sessions*, directed by Bernard MacMahon, showed Elton taking a Taupin lyric, "Two Fingers of Whiskey," and knocking it up into a finished song with the help of Jack White and T Bone Burnett. The process took minutes, giving a valuable insight into Elton's rapid-fire working methods. But the year ended on a sad note, as Sheila, Elton's mother, died on December 4, aged ninety-two.

Solace lay in the fact that they'd recently reconciled after a falling-out in 2008. It seems a petty disagreement then had fractured their relationship, which had of course seen her both ignite and support his musical endeavors in earlier days. The row had come when he'd asked her to break off her friendships with John Reid (his former manager and lover) and Bob Halley (his former driver and personal assistant for thirty years, who'd resigned after disagreements).

More happily, they had at least made up earlier in 2017. It took a calamity to cause them both to drop the bickering. On April 22, Elton was taken to hospital after contracting an "unusual" and dangerous bacterial infection during a flight home from a Santiago, Chile, leg of a South American tour. He was

WONDERFUL CRAZY NIGHT

TRACK LIST
Wonderful Crazy Night
In the Name of You
Claw Hammer
Blue Wonderful
I've Got 2 Wings
A Good Heart
Looking Up
Guilty Pleasure
Tambourine
The Open Chord
Bonus Tracks
Free and Easy
England and America

Recorded at the Village, Los Angeles, USA
Produced by T Bone Burnett & Elton John
Released February 5, 2016
Label Mercury, 4765082
Highest chart position on release UK 6, US 8, CAN 18, AUS 11, FRA 35, ITA 15, GER 10, NOR 17, SPA 32

KEY PERSONNEL
Elton John: piano, lead vocals
Kim Bullard: keyboards
Davey Johnstone: guitar, harmony vocals
Matt Bissonette: bass guitar, harmony vocals
Nigel Olsson: drums, harmony vocals
John Mahon: percussion, harmony vocals

COVER ART
Mat Maitland: art direction & design
Joseph Guay and Juergen Teller: photography

forced to cancel two months of shows, and the situation seemed worrying. "Potentially deadly," wrote the *Los Angeles Times*. Thankfully, he was discharged after two nights in intensive care.

This put matters into perspective. The silly disputes were shelved. Elton posted photos of himself with Sheila on Instagram, adding, "Dear Mum, Happy Mother's Day! So happy we are back in touch. Love, Elton x." When she died, he wrote on Facebook, "So sad to say that my mother passed away this morning. I only saw her last Monday and am in shock. Travel safe, Mum. Thank you for everything." Sheila had certainly experienced a more interesting journey than most, from bringing home Elvis and Bill Haley records for her son to enjoy in Northwood Hills to seeing him explode as one of the world's most famous entertainers. Her recent loss may have influenced the dewy-eyed sentiments of the 2018 John Lewis Christmas commercial.

Her Reggie remained an entertainer prone to tantrums and insulting those who adored him. In Las Vegas in March 2018,

LEFT: Onstage at Palau Sant Jordi in Barcelona, Spain, December 2017, as part of the Wonderful Crazy Night tour.
ABOVE: Live at Sunset Open Air in Zurich, Switzerland, July 2017.

midway through "Saturday Night's Alright for Fighting," one of the audience members that he'd invited onstage started touching him, attempting to play the piano, trying to take pictures, and high-fiving him. Swearing at the overzealous fan, Elton stopped playing, and left the stage. He did return to perform "Circle of Life," but unceremoniously warned the crowd that audience members would no longer be allowed onstage.

Whether this incident was related to a recent announcement he'd made is debatable. For Elton had, in January, revealed that he would be retiring from touring. But not just yet. There was to be an epic farewell tour, spanning the next three years, going under the name Farewell Yellow Brick Road. And in September, this extended victory lap began in Allentown, Pennsylvania. He cited the classic motive for retirement: wanting to spend more time with his family. "Ten years ago," he was reported as saying by *Deadline*, "If you'd asked me if I would stop touring, I'd have said no. But we had children—and that changed our lives. I have

had an amazing life and career, but my life has changed. My priorities are now my children and my husband and my family." He'd turned seventy-one in March 2018. You could understand his reasoning. It wasn't like he'd ever been reticent in putting himself out there, on stages around the world.

Still, the big final hurrah was to be quite a marathon. And as the tour trekked across the planet, bringing audiences to a sort of last-chance rapture, it felt as if Elton's profile had never been higher. It also felt as if, aware of his legacy, he was taking care to curate it.

As for Bernie, who turned sixty-eight in May 2018, he's still living on a California ranch near Santa Ynez, married to his fourth wife. After three divorces, he's been with Heather Kidd since 2004. They have two daughters, Charlie Indiana and Georgey Devon. The Kid has kids. He's written songs for everyone from Courtney Love to Brian Wilson, and—finding vindication away from Elton—won a Golden Globe for his lyrics

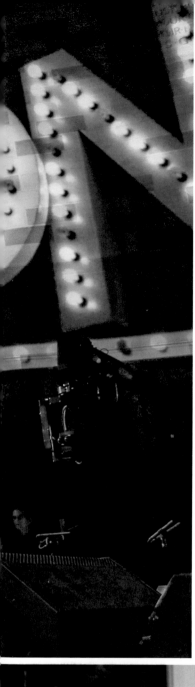

to "A Love That Will Never Grow Old" from the 2005 film *Brokeback Mountain.* Yet it's an undeniable fact that he'll always be primarily thought of for his decades-long creative bond with the Captain.

As Elton stays almost daily in the news, whether it's mourning Aretha Franklin or partying with the Beckhams, he's still, as Kiki Dee would have it, got the music in him. With a new UMG deal signed that gold-seals his financial fortunes, he's featured on an album by Nile Rodgers singing a duet with Emeli Sandé, sent himself up surrounded by rappers in a Snickers ad, and of course reminded generations of their soft spot for him in that John Lewis Christmas commercial.

As the farewell tour rolls on, with Elton swiftly bouncing back from an ear infection causing cancellations in America, rumors persist that he might mount a glorious British swansong by playing at Glastonbury in 2020. At the time of writing, these remain just rumors. Established as truth are his ongoing

endeavors raising AIDS awareness, with huge funds being garnered by his efforts around every World AIDS Day. He's moved into the age of social media smoothly, his Instagram photos showing a selection of concert and offstage shots, warming up appetites for when his show reaches your town.

His legacy, fifty years on from his debut album, *Empty Sky*, has been further burnished by the movie *Rocketman*, from Paramount Pictures, which hit screens in May 2019. Covering his crazy days of the seventies and eighties, it is directed by Dexter Fletcher, who also helmed *Bohemian Rhapsody*, the Queen/Freddie Mercury biopic. Retaining control over cinematic representation, Elton and David are among the producers, and the screenplay is by Lee "Billy Elliot" Hall. Taron Egerton, who'd met Elton on the set of the *Kingsman* movie, plays him. Early scenes at the time of this writing showed the young piano player excelling at the Royal Academy of Music, and meeting and working with Bernie was shown as key to his career. Like the Queen movie, though, the film aims for the most part to be a colorful, fun celebration laced with fantasy-musical elements, while not completely whitewashing the excess and chemical indulgences of the era in question. It doesn't skimp on scenes of exuberance and costumes to match. Also appearing are Jamie Bell (the actor who originally played Billy Elliot) as Bernie, Richard Madden as John Reid, and Bryce Dallas Howard as Sheila, Elton's mum.

Whether you enjoy the film greatly depends on your response to the performance of Taron Egerton in the role of young Elton. (A few years earlier, Elton had named Justin Timberlake as his first choice to play him, and Tom Hardy was also in line for the role for a while.) Egerton brings plenty of youthful energy, and

he'd taken singing lessons. He told the *Collider* website he had tried "to create some semblance of a performance that is at least reminiscent of him." He emphasized that the film about Elton's formative years was about "fun." "Everyone thinks it's a biopic: it isn't," he protested. "It's a fantasy musical so it's actually his songs used to express important beats in his life at emotional moments. He's not the only character that sings." Researching the role, he'd visited Elton's home, read his diaries, and was "scared everyone's going to hate me." He was glad Elton didn't watch him shooting some crucial scenes. "Playing him is intimidating enough. Particularly given the fact that it's a fairly warts-and-all story. I shot a scene where I'm him losing his virginity: I didn't particularly want to do that while the person I'm playing is watching. That would be weird. On many levels."

Elton Hercules John's whole life and career have been weird—and fantastic—on many levels. From his Pinner beginnings and early struggles to shine, through overnight Stateside success to his enduring place at the peak of pop's pantheon, he's defied logic and expectation, making virtues of his failings, strengths of his weaknesses. Across rock's glory years and into the modern era, he's stayed interested and interesting. As the valedictory address of his farewell tour weaves its way around an admiring planet, this rocket man's boosters are still burning.

LEFT: Performing during his Farewell Yellow Brick Road tour at the BB&T Center, Sunrise, Florida, November 23, 2018.
ABOVE: Taron Egerton stars as Elton John in *Rocketman*, 2019.
NEXT PAGE: In concert, Farewell Yellow Brick Road tour, SAP Center, San Jose, California, January 19, 2019.

GREYSCALE

BIN TRAVELER FORM

Cut By ___Sinku___ Qty ___14___ Date __09/13/24__

Scanned By ___Camren Q___ Qty ___14___ Date __9/14/24__

Scanned Batch IDs

___T409234D1___ ___T409232608___

Notes / Exception

Daily Book Scanning Log

Name: ꞓamoꞑ Ɋ uꞥuꞥ   Date: 9/19/24   # of Scanners: 2

BIN #	BOOKS COMPLETED	# OF PAGES	NOTES / EXCEPTIONS
Bin 1	17	6312	
Bin 2	14		
Bin 3			
Bin 4			
Bin 5			
Bin 6			
Bin 7			
Bin 8			
Bin 9			
Bin 10			
Bin 11			
Bin 12			
Bin 13			
Bin 14			
Bin 15			
Bin 16			
Bin 17			
Bin 18			
Bin 19			
Bin 20			
Bin 21			
Bin 22			
Bin 23			
Bin 24			
Bin 25			
Bin 26			
Bin 27			
Bin 28			
Bin 29			
Bin 30			
Bin 31			
Bin 32			
Bin 33			
Bin 34			
Bin 35			
Bin 36			
Bin 37			
Bin 38			
Bin 39			
Bin 40			